AN ILLUSTRATED HISTORY OF HACKNEY

STRENGTH IN THE TOWER

DAVID MANDER

SUTTON PUBLISHING

LONDON BOROUGH OF HACKNEY

Sutton Publishing Limited
Phoenix Mill · Thrupp · Stroud
Gloucestershire · GL5 2BU

First published 1998

Title page photograph: Hackney's first town hall, dating from 1802, had ceased to be the seat of local government by the date of this George James photograph of about 1870, but housed a range of local institutions, including the Hackney Bank for Savings.

British Library Cataloguing in Publication Data
A catalogue record for this book is available from the British Library.

ISBN 0-7509-1759-8

Typesetting and origination by
Sutton Publishing Limited.
Printed in Great Britain by
Ebenezer Baylis, Worcester.

Cover photograph: Hackney's old church tower rises above the Old Town Hall, Mare Street. Photograph, Alfred Braddock, *c.* 1900.

For Carole and Mike: a piece of Hackney for the future

Acknowledgements
All pictures are from the LB Hackney Archives Department, except for the following, for whose use I would like to thank the following individuals and organisations: the maps on pp. iv and 41, drawn by K.J. Wass, the Victoria History of the Counties of England; p. 2, the Sutton House Society, via the National Trust; p. 4, Hackney Museum; p. 12, Professor Elaine Murphy; p. 22, Museum of London, Guildhall Library Maps and Prints Department; p. 81, London Metropolitan Archives; p. 109, LB Hackney Regulatory Services; and p. 199, National Trust. In addition, special thanks are due to Tim Baker, Mike Gray, Raymond Lee, Martin Taylor and Isobel Watson for research, past and present.

Builders pause in their labours in Clapton Passage in the summer of 1882. The bowler-hatted man with the wooden leg may be Christopher Ruthven, who applied for consent to connect the new houses to Hackney's sewers. Photograph, Alfred Braddock.

CONTENTS

Due to economic constraints, the sources for this book have unfortunately been omitted. A copy is available from the Hackney Archives and can be inspected in the Local History Collection.

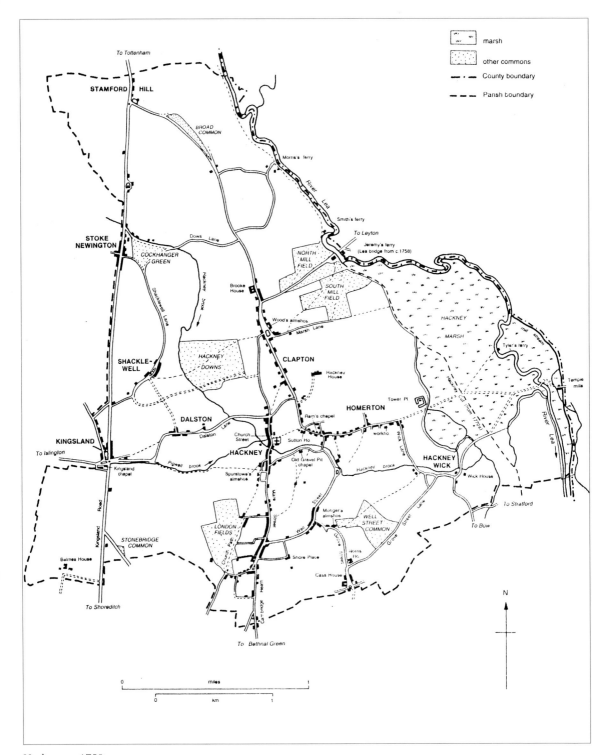

To Tottenham

STAMFORD HILL

BROAD COMMON

Morris's ferry

River Lea

Smith's ferry

STOKE NEWINGTON

Dows Lane

COCKHANGER GREEN

To Leyton

Jeremy's ferry (Lea bridge from c 1758)

NORTH MILL FIELD

Brooke House

SOUTH MILL FIELD

Hackney brook

Shacklewell Lane

Wood's almshos

HACKNEY MARSH

Marsh Lane

SHACKLE-WELL

HACKNEY DOWNS

CLAPTON

Tyler's ferry

Hackney House

Temple mills

DALSTON

Dalston Lane

HOMERTON

Tower Pl

Ram's chapel

workho

KINGSLAND

Church Street

Sutton Ho

Wick Lane

To Islington

Kingsland chapel

Pigwell brook

HACKNEY

Old Gravel Pit chapel

Hackney brook

HACKNEY WICK

Wick House

Spurstowe's almshos

To Stratford

Monger's almshos

WELL STREET COMMON

To Bow

Kingsland Road

Balmes House

STONEBRIDGE COMMON

LONDON FIELDS

Well Street

Grove Street Lane

Norris Ho

Shore Place

Cass House

Church Fields

Cambridge Heath

To Shoreditch

To Bethnal Green

N

miles
0   1

km
0   1

Hackney, *c.* 1750.

1. INTRODUCTION

Today's Hackney is one of the London boroughs formed in 1965, made up of three former Middlesex parishes; Stoke Newington, Shoreditch and Hackney itself. It is with the older Hackney that this history is principally concerned. Totalling some 3,300 acres, Hackney was the largest parish in the old county of Middlesex. Attractively rural before the middle of the nineteenth century, yet close to the city of London, it was home to courtiers and wealthy Londoners. Hackney has also had a long association with radicals and dissent and its inhabitants have made considerable contributions to national as well as local history. For this third volume in the series that tells the story of the three component parts of modern Hackney, a variation on the motto that accompanied the old metropolitan borough coat of arms provides the title. Hackney's original motto was *Justitia nostra turris* – justice is our tower – but I have chosen to emphasize fortitude rather than the law in keeping with the old church tower itself: Hackney's oldest surviving building, which outlasted the church of which it was once a part and which has resisted neglect and adversity.

There are no firm population estimates before the census of 1801. In 1524 there were 156 people assessed for the subsidy – a tax – of 1524, making Hackney comparatively populous. In 1548 there were 600 communicants, while 195 landholders and a further 29 non-residents were asked to pay the church rates in 1605. The distribution of those resident landholders gives a rough impression of relative densities of population. There were forty-nine in Homerton, thirty-four in Church Street, twenty-three in Mare Street, twenty-four in Well Street and Grove Street combined and thirty-three in Newington – the combination of Dalston, Kingsland and Shacklewell. Homerton's larger figure reflects the higher status the area enjoyed in the sixteenth and early seventeenth centuries. By 1640 there were some 324 households, rising to 388 houses either liable or exempt from hearth tax in 1664, though of the 305 liable properties, 27 were empty. By 1672 the house total had risen to 462, though there were only 448 householders and a further 25 living elsewhere in 1720. The figure for 1735 was 658 and 15 outsiders. House numbers steadily climbed from 983 in 1756 to 1,212 in 1779, over 1,500 in 1789 and 2,050 in 1801, when the population stood at 12,730.

The 1801 figures give an estimated figure of six people per house. If this figure is taken as a very rough guide to likely population numbers – and it would have to be very rough as not all inhabitants would have been permanent residents – this would give the following figures: 1640, 1944; 1664, 2,166 (excluding empty properties); 1720, 2,772 (total house figures); 1735, 3,948; 1756, 5,898; 1779, 7,272; 1789, 9,000 plus; 1801, 12,730 (actual). The sharply rising figures of the later eighteenth century bear some correlation with the rising numbers and cost of local paupers and contributed to the pressure on the church of St John at Hackney and its burial ground. But in 1806 two-thirds of the parish remained farmland

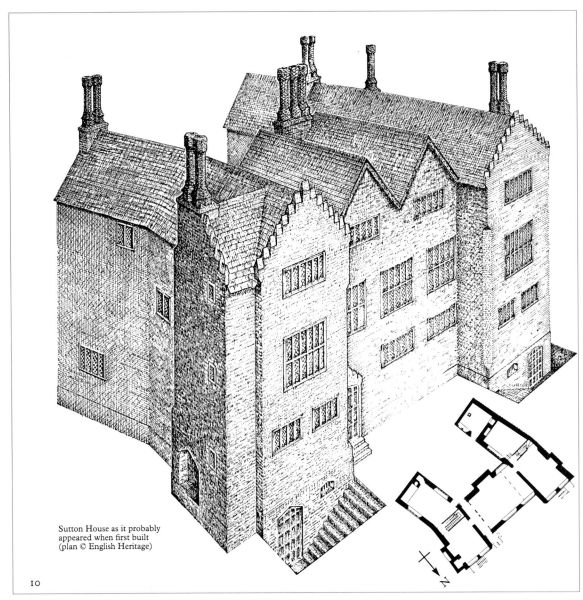

Sutton House as it probably
appeared when first built
(plan © English Heritage)

10

N

Sutton House is Hackney's oldest surviving domestic building. This reconstructed image by Richard Bond shows Ralph Sadleir's 'bryk place' as it would have appeared shortly after construction in 1535.

and of that 1,500 acres, about 45 per cent of the total of 3,300 acres, was grass and marshland. In 1751 it was possible for a hunt to travel across open land and fields in pursuit a stag, which they chased all the way from Epping, through Walthamstow, over the Lea at Brazier's Ferry and across Hackney until the animal was unable to get over a wall in Brick Lane.

2. MANORS, ESTATES & CHURCH (TO 1660)

Hackney lies on a mixture of gravel, clay, brick-earth and alluvial deposits. Alluvium lies along the Lea and under Hackney Marsh on the east. Brick-earth lies beneath Stamford Hill and Clapton Common, bounded on either side by tongues of London clay, which extend a little to the south of Hackney Downs. Towards the centre and the west are beds of Taplow gravel, covering much of the remainder of the parish, except the area round Well Street Common and Victoria Park, which are on flood plain gravel. The highest point in the parish is thirty-three metres, near the junction of Portland Avenue and Stamford Hill, with steep descents to the Lea and High Hill Ferry and a gentler slope on Spring Hill. Clapton Common is mainly above twenty-five metres, with Lower Clapton about five metres lower. Victoria Park is below fifteen metres and parts of Hackney Wick fall below ten metres.

There is little record of pre-Roman settlers in the area. Despite the presence of Ermine Street on the western side of the parish, no Roman structures have been found. Stone coffins have been discovered in Springfield Park in the early nineteenth century and a marble sarcophagus at Lower Clapton. It is possible that the pottery and burial finds at Springfield Park may relate to a lost Roman villa but no evidence has as yet come to light. Coins in an urn found near Temple Mills may have been concealed alongside a lost crossing point of the Lea.

The Saxons have left their mark on local place-names. The parish name is first recorded in 1198 but is likely to derive from 'Hacas *ey*', a raised place in a marsh. The derivation of 'hackney' for a type of horse is thought to be unconnected with the parish name. The 'tuns' in Dalston, Homerton and Clapton are all from the Old English for farm, named respectively from Deorlaf, a woman called Hunburh and from the Old English '*clop*', a lump or hill (and so making Clapton the farm on the hill). The '*wic*' of Hackney Wick refers to a house or settlement, possibly a dairy farm. Mare Street does not have any equine associations either, as it is probably derived from Middle English '*mere*' or boundary, possibly suggesting an early settlement or a piece of water – in this case lying at the south end of the road near Cambridge Heath. Shacklewell is from the Old English '*sceacel*', to shackle or fetter, though the link with a local spring or well is uncertain. Stamford Hill was *Saumforthill* in 1382, the hill by the sandy ford (over the Hackney Brook). Hackney's southern settlement at Grove Street, the present Lauriston Road, is possibly named from a grove that may have stretched westward from the present Lauriston Road to Shore Road.

Physical Saxon remains are rarer. Most of their structures would have left little but post holes behind and to date the only significant remains have been preserved by waterlogging. A six metre clinker-built boat was found during the construction of the waterworks south of Lea Bridge in the mid-1830s, although archaeological techniques of the day were unable to date it.

Archaeologists from the Museum of London's
Archaeological Service test a replica of the
Anglo-Saxon log boat, 1988.

A large portion of an oak dug-out from about AD 950 was uncovered during excavations for a playground at Big Hill in 1987. The boat was carefully dried out by the Museum of London and will form a significant exhibit in Hackney's new museum.

By late Saxon times Hackney formed part of the manor of Stepney and has no separate entry in the Domesday of 1086. However it is possible that the four hides (roughly 320 acres) held by Robert Fafiton may have corresponded to the later Kingshold manor. Fafiton's holdings had land for three ploughs, within which a hide of land belonged to Roger the sheriff. Two villeins had a further twenty-six acres and a further three virgates (or about sixty acres) were divided among an uncounted number of smallholders. There was woodland for sixty pigs. Stepney had belonged to the Bishops of London from the early seventh century. The manorial customs were defined in a codifying Parliamentary act of 1736.

Descent among manorial tenants was by gavelkind, where a tenant's estate was either divided among the sons or in default by the daughters, with the youngest co-heir having first choice. By 1623 specific tenants also had other benefits, which included the rights to fell trees, dig the waste in front of their houses, and not repair their houses or make short leases for up to thirty-one years, four months. These terms, which were compatible with agricultural use, were to be a considerable hindrance to intending building developers from the mid-eighteenth century onwards.

By 1386 the separate Hackney accounts show that only a few meadows were retained by the lord, while the remainder were leased out, including parts of the demesne, or the lord's own holding. Rents from both arable and pasture rose after the Black Death in the 1380s and 1390s but dropped sharply in the depressed years of the early fifteenth century. The rentals of 1386 also show that the Bishop of London was taking hay from Hackney to Stepney and for his own use – hay was the medieval equivalent of petrol, needed quite literally for horsepower. Most medieval records of animals refer to cattle but Geoffrey Davy (d. *c.* 1299) had a flock of a hundred sheep at Hackney Wick. On the Templars' Hackney estate in 1185, the terms of landholding included the provision of a man or men for the hay harvest. Corn was being bought in in the 1380s and there is little record of arable land. Wick manor supported twenty-six cattle and four horses in 1400, while the Hospitallers' lands were mainly pasture at the Dissolution. By the early seventeenth century the only remaining arable was at Hackney Downs.

By 1652 the demesne of Hackney manor consisted of the 138 or so acres of Scotland Farm, another 30 acres south of Homerton, 6 acres on Millfields Lane and a further 64 acres in dispersed strips in Hackney Marsh. In common with the majority of riverside parishes, Hackney tenants would all have once held strips in Hackney Marsh in addition to their holdings in higher and dryer parts of the parish. The marsh formed part of the commonable parish lands, on which tenants enjoyed rights of pasturage from 1 August (Lammas, hence the 'Lammas lands'). Besides the marsh these comprised Hackney Downs, London Fields, Well Street Common and the Millfields. The majority of later regulations concerned the marsh, which was defined in 1185 as being divided into the '*humbra*' or marshy meadows and the '*quabba*' or bog.

'*Quab*' and derivatives were still being used as part of field names in the eighteenth century. The 1623 act confirmed the annual appointment of manorial drovers and fines for the impounding of stray beasts. The marsh itself was divided into strips, some 283 of them as mapped in 1745. By that date the lord of the manor held seventy-two acres but only six other holdings exceeded ten acres, the majority being below five acres. Strip division also applied to Millfields and Hackney Downs as late as the mid-eighteenth century. There were larger divisions on Well Street Common by 1700 and on London Fields at the end of the eighteenth century. Stoke Newington Common was owned by the lords of the manor but common pasturage was allowed throughout the year.

The substitution of rents for the majority of bonded labour duties did not mean the manors lost their importance, either as regulatory bodies or as pieces of property. In 1294 the Bishop of London claimed a range of rights which included the assize of bread and ale, fugitives' goods, tumbril, pillory, gallows and fines (for the transfer of land on the death of a tenant or for breaches of tenure). Manorial court records survive for Stepney from 1380, sometimes with Hackney pleas entered separately. By 1509 two officers, probably the constables, were elected for Hackney and two chief pledgers or headboroughs elected for Shacklewell and one each for Clapton and Homerton. By the 1580s the constables had been joined by two aletasters, three common drovers and six headboroughs (two for Clapton, two for Mare Street, Well Street and Grove Street and the remaining two for Dalston, Kingsland, Shacklewell and Newington). Manorial courts tried to ensure ditches were kept clean, bread was sold by the correct weights, and law and order maintained. By 1605 there were overlapping areas of responsibility between parish and manor, notably on control of the commons, while the parish instructed the constable on the regulation of the poor in 1618 before the office of beadle was created. Gradually the parish took over the former local government functions of the manor, although manorial regulation of commons continued into the nineteenth century and, faced with parliamentary election expenses in 1833, the parish was quick to repudiate any connection with manorial officers.

Hackney manor was first separated from Stepney in 1550 when it was granted to the Wentworth family. Mortgaged in 1632 by Thomas Wentworth, Earl of Cleveland, it was forfeited for Royalist support in 1650 and purchased by Richard Blackwell, treasurer of prize goods, in 1653. Thereafter it was in the hands of successive rich Londoners, including William Hobson in 1660, followed by two who were later lord mayors, William Bolton and Patience Ward. Bolton, Ward and William White came to terms with the Wentworth family over the legality of their title and the manor was sold

Thomas Wentworth, Earl of Cleveland.

successively to an alderman, John Forth, and then in 1675 to two goldsmiths, Nicholas Cary and Thomas Cooke. Their assigns and widow sold it to Francis Tyssen the elder, a naturalized merchant from Flushing, in 1697. By this stage a name was required to distinguish it from other Hackney manors, all of which were to come into the hands of the Tyssens, and it became Lordshold.

There is no known manor house for Lordshold, though the house at Shacklewell was used by the Tyssens and came to be known as the Manor House. The Manor House on Church Street (now the Narrow Way, Mare Street) was not built until about 1845 and took its name from J.R.D. Tyssen, who served as steward to the manor, but this was the first association of the site with matters manorial.

Hackney's second manor grew from the holdings in the parish of the Knights Templars, who were given an estate in the reign of Henry II by the king's steward William of Hastings, later known as Hastingmede. This was augmented by land from one Ailbrith, which they granted to Robert of Wick, and from this came the supposed manor of Wick. Its status is questionable as no manorial courts have ever been traced for the Wick and it is the exercise of rights through a court that distinguishes a manor from a mere landholding. By 1307 the Templars' holding comprised 35½ acres in Hackney, a further 9 acres in Leyton and two mills, and this passed to the Hospitallers on the suppression of the Templars in 1312. The Hospitallers were one of the orders dissolved by Henry VIII and their lands passed to the Crown, from which arose the later name of Kingshold. The manor was sold to two Londoners, Thomas Banks and Thomas Land in 1614, though the mills were exempted from the sale. The manor was purchased by the same William Hobson who was later to buy Lordshold, though his Kingshold acquisition was made in 1647. After his death in 1662 his heirs and executors sold it to Sir George Vyner in 1668. Vyner's heirs sold it on after his death in 1673 to John Sikes, a London merchant, and it was Sikes who sold it to Tyssen in 1697.

The house that is normally linked with Lordshold manor was the Hospitallers' property on the north side of Well Street. Known as the Pilgrims House, in 1415 it had been the home of Richard Pande, servant and 'charioteer' of the Bishop of London. In 1693 it had its own orchard and garden next to the site of the former manorial pound. A drawing of 1741 shows it with a two-storey courtyard built of chequered brick and decorated with a cross. The former moat had been filled in. Like so many of Hackney's early houses it rapidly descended down the social scale in the eighteenth century, having been subdivided among poor tenants, including chimney-sweeps, before 1795. It had probably been demolished before 1810 and the surmise that it had been a house of the prior of St John survived in the name St John's Place for houses built on the site. Like many another Johnian associations, the 'saint' was transformed into a king and the building became one of the legion of spurious 'King John's Palaces' that populated the nineteenth-century English imagination.

A house on the east side of Church Street near the site of the present Crown public house was known as the Templars' House, though it spent most of the last century of its life as a tavern called the Blue Posts. The outside of the building was adorned with ionic pilasters, although an earlier drawing shows these to have been an addition to a building that was once adorned with sixteenth-century style cupolas on its three projecting bays. There is no proven association of Templars with the site and it is more likely that the house was built for one of Hackney's wealthy incomers in the later fifteenth or early sixteenth century. An assembly room added in the mid-eighteenth century survived the demolition of the house in about 1814.

One part of Kingshold manor was claimed as a manor in its own right, although the claim was never properly substantiated. This was the estate at Clapton attached to another estate later called

The Templars' House showing the original turrets, an undated drawing

... and around 1820, after alteration.

Brooke House, *c*. 1844. Watercolour by G.W. Toussaint.

the King's Place or Brooke House. The earliest this has been traced back with certainty is to Sir William Estfield, another London alderman, who sold it in about 1439 to William Booth, rector of Hackney and later Archbishop of York. In 1476 it passed by marriage to a relative of Booth's, William Worsley, Dean of St Paul's, who sold it in 1496 to Sir Reginald Bray. It passed by sale and marriage to successive courtiers until Sir Thomas Neville, then Speaker of the House of Commons, whose wife had inherited it, sold it to Henry Percy, Earl of Northumberland in about 1531. Percy built up large debts and these forced him to surrender the estate to the Crown in 1535.

The royal tenure was not lengthy. In 1547 the estate was granted to Sir William Herbert, later Earl of Pembroke, and after a brief period when they were held by Sir Ralph Sadleir, the builder of Sutton House, they passed to the Carew family (1547–78), Henry Carey, Lord Hunsdon (1578–83), Sir Rowland Hayward, twice Lord Mayor of London, and in 1596 to Elizabeth, Countess of Oxford. Her husband, Edward de Vere, Earl of Oxford, credited by some with being the author of Shakespeare's plays, was resident there from 1596 until his death in 1604. The countess later sold her interest in the estate to Fulke Grenville, later Baron Brooke, in 1609 and it was the Baron whose title gave the house its best-known name. The Brookes, who later became earls of Warwick, kept the estate until 1819 when it too was sold to the Tyssens.

Brooke House may have begun as the dean's hall on Worsley's estate. After it was acquired for Henry VIII in 1535, Thomas Cromwell carried out major building works that created a quadrangular house and it was in this form that the King's Place provided the venue for Henry's reconciliation with his daughter Mary in 1536. It was further repaired before the transfer of 1547 to Herbert, when it included a hall, a parlour, a large gallery, chapel and library and was surrounded by a large ditch. Lord Hunsdon carried out major building works in about 1580, adding his coat of arms to the ceiling decorations of the extensive first floor gallery. Later alterations closed the original 'E' plan to make two courtyards.

Margaret, Countess of Lennox, used the house before her death in 1578 and Queen Elizabeth I was a visitor in 1583 and 1587. The house was tenanted by 1716 and it was in use as a lunatic asylum from 1760 until 1940. Alterations included the creation of a Georgian frontage to Upper Clapton Road and the division of the long gallery in the nineteenth century. Bomb damage to the older parts in 1940 and again in 1944 sealed its fate and after sale to the LCC in that year, the remains were cleared away ten years later.

The right to appoint the rector of Hackney was vested in the Bishop of London until 1550. With the rectory went the rectory estate which may have formed part of an estate of one Daniel in 1349, which by 1384 was known as Daniels, now Grumbolds. The latter name, which may come from an early thirteenth-century Hackney family, became the usual name for what had become the rectory manor by the seventeenth century. These families would have leased from the rector, who would usually have been an absentee.

From 1540 the farmer (or lessee) of the manor was Sir Thomas Heneage. A series of sixteenth-century lessees culminated in John Daniell, who surrendered the manor and the rectory house in lieu of a very heavy fine in 1601, but was still imprisoned and had his ears cropped. Daniell's wife, Jane, a daughter of a former governor of Ghent, had been a servant of the Countess of Essex and the pair had had access to some compromising letters, which Daniell intended to use for extortion. Jane Daniell drew up an inventory of their possessions left in the gatehouse of the parsonage when the Daniells and their servants were evicted by Ralph Bell; this provides a glimpse of some of the possessions of Hackney's upper classes in the sixteenth century. Among her pearl ornaments was 'a stone ringe for the spleene', a cyprus comb and a pair of 'corell brasletts'. Her clothes included 'cambrick handerkerchieves' with laid work of gold and silver; two pairs of gloves, one pair decorated with gold and silver silk arras work; a variety of stomachers, with silk decorations in gold and black; crimson and scarlet satin petticoats, one guarded with velvet; taffeta and holland waistcoats; holland smocks; a variety of gowns, including a 'Tufted Taffata gowne wrought in starres color blacke and a black tufted Taffata Kyrtle to that gowne', which perhaps went with 'a little crymasyn taffata Cloake lyned with armens'. Her linen also included 'a Cambrycke sheate for a woman in chyldbed', while her kitchenware contained a range of pewterware which comprised dishes, salt-cellars, candlesticks, spoons and a chamber-pot; a leather-covered close stool, a bushel measure, three sieves to dress corn and 'a greate drye Fatte [vat] to powder hogges in'. There was little food left but the list included six flitches of bacon and three 'rowles of grease'.

Patronage of the rectory and the manor of Grumbolds was separated from Hackney manor in 1647 when the Earl of Cleveland sold them through an intermediary to William Stephens. Thomas Fowkes bought the rectory in 1654 and the tithes had passed to William Hobson by 1664. Fowkes and the Wentworths (as heirs of the Earl of Cleveland) sold their interests to John Forth, who in turn sold on to Daniel Farrington in 1675. Five years later Farrington sold them on to Thomas Cooke and Nicholas Cary, and they were included in the sale to Tyssen in 1697.

Daniel was resident at the rectory house but later rectors leased the house and glebe lands to the patron. Unlike the manors of Lordshold and Kingshold, Grumbolds manor was fairly compact, running along both sides of Church Street. The rectory house itself stood behind the west side of the street, together with the glebe field of five acres. The land had an orchard and a fishpond in 1580 and barns in 1622. The house was converted into cottages and demolished in 1845 when J.R.D. Tyssen built the new manor house.

Although the connection between the Templars and the house named after them on Church Street is unproven, the Templars did hold land at Hackney Wick, which they acquired when the previous tenant, Ailbrith, entered their order. It had been granted to Richard of Wick by the master of the order in 1185. When their order was dissolved the Templars' holdings passed to the Hospitallers and successive leases of the estate included London aldermen. In 1349 it consisted of two houses and 114 acres at the Wick. In the late fourteenth century it passed through marriage to the Montagu earls of Salisbury and remained with the earldom until the death in battle of Richard Neville, earl both of Salisbury and of Warwick, in 1471; then it passed to the Crown. Leased out, it was briefly in the hands of Margaret, Countess of Salisbury, who sold it in 1538 to William Bowyer, later knighted and a lord mayor of London. Bowyer's heirs had sold it by 1602 to Benedict Haynes, whose second heir sold it in 1633 to John Bayliffe.

There may have been a chief house at the Wick as early as 1399. One existed in 1566 and was either replaced or substantially rebuilt by John Bayliffe. This passed to the Clobbery family by inheritance and had twenty hearths in 1664. It stood on the east side of the present Eastway, not far

The grounds of the New Mermaid, once part of the original Hackney rectory's glebe lands. The assembly room is the large building just below the church tower, and the old rectory is in the centre with the chimneys of the Spurstowe house rising above it in this 1811 view over the wall from the site of the present Kenmure Road on the occasion of a balloon ascent.

from the site of the Victoria public house. After the death of Henry Clobbery in 1665 the estate passed to his executor and then by successive sales to Edward Woodcock, a lawyer, who sold it to Joseph Barbaroux in 1753. Ten years later Woodcock bought back most of it, though not the house, pleasure grounds, mill house and field to the north. Thereafter estate and house were sold separately. William Gilbee bought the estate from the Woodcock family in 1796 and the Gilbees retained it until 1831, when part was sold to the developer William Bradshaw. Mary Anne Bradshaw acquired the remainder in 1866, by which time development was well under way. Wick House was rebuilt after 1760 and was in Gilbee's hands by 1809, when it was leased to astronomer Mark Beaufoy, whose son Henry left a record of his scientific observations made during a balloon journey from the Wick out into Essex in 1811. It was in use as Wick Hall Collegiate School from 1841 and demolished in about 1862.

Another reputed manor was Shoreditch Place in South Hackney. There was a house called De La Grave on a site at the rear of the present 18 Shore Place in 1319, when John of Bodley sold it to John and Maud Borewell. Maud and her second husband sold it in 1324 to Sir John of Shoreditch, Baron of the Exchequer, and his wife Ellen. Sir John and his brother Nicholas went on to add several other properties in Hackney to their holdings and also leased a house called Beaulieu in the parish from the Hospitallers. Robert Shoreditch leased out twenty-one acres of the estate in 1473 to Simon Elrington, whose family built a chantry chapel in Shoreditch church and re-established a guild in Hackney church. More land was settled on John and Henry Tey from 1478 after George Shoreditch married Elizabeth Tey, including the Grove House (presumably the earlier De La Grave). William Tey surrendered a house of 147 acres of land at Hackney to the Crown in 1513, and four years later it passed to the hospital of the Savoy, created in 1505. The hospital's other holdings included six acres in London Fields (together with a toft house or land where a house once stood) called Barber's Barn, site of the later sixteenth-century house and which was leased from the Hospitallers. However the Savoy was to be short-lived, for it was dissolved in 1553 and its Hackney holdings passed to St Thomas Hospital.

By 1628 the bulk of the hospital's Hackney lands lay in three blocks; one south of Well Street, the second south of Morning Lane and the third at Upper Clapton. The estate was leased out to a single tenant in the seventeenth century and one tenant, Sir Thomas Player, secured an extension in 1671 following his

Balmes House, south-west front. Watercolour by G.W. Toussaint, 1852.

rebuilding of Bowling Green House (whose successor was on the east side of Chatham Place). The whole estate was leased out to builders in the nineteenth century. The majority of the freehold interests were disposed of after 1931.

An archaeological excavation in 1978 uncovered the foundations of an early medieval house. This had two barns, stables and a dovehouse in 1504 and was rebuilt by the hospital's tenant William Cross after 1612. In 1628 it was a castellated building of five bays with its own orchard and approach from a drive on the line of the present Shore Road. Storm damage in about 1661 claimed the crenellations and the house name changed from Shoreditch Place in 1697 to Shore Place or House in the eighteenth century. It was probably then that the spurious associations with Jane Shore, mistress of Edward IV, were made. By the early eighteenth century the house was leased out annually and probably divided; tenants included Robert Billio, minister at the Mare Street meeting house, and cousin of the diarist Dudley Ryder. By 1720 it was in poor repair; ten years later it was shown as a three-storey house and survived until it formed part of a lease granted to speculator Thomas Flight in 1768. Flight demolished the old house and his new buildings included another Shore House on the same site. This in turn was wholly rebuilt in the late 1980s.

The area of much of the modern De Beauvoir Town once formed part of another reputed manor, called Hoxton or Balmes. The boundary with Shoreditch was not settled until 1697, when the area came within Hackney. In 1305, when Robert of Aspley bought the estate, it consisted of a house, a mill, 167 acres of land and rents of other property. It passed through the hands of several Londoners, including Adam Bamme, who acquired it when his wife's father died in 1389. Bamme, like his father-in-law Sir John Philpot, was a lord mayor of London. The Philpot family retained the estate, Bams or Balmes, until 1634 when it was bought by Sir William Whitmore. Whitmore's father, a haberdasher, held the lease of the estate on his death in 1593 and at the time of the purchase it consisted of a house, a cottage, two gardens, an orchard and 153 acres divided between Hackney, Shoreditch and Tottenham. Sir William had bought the estate on behalf of his younger brother Sir George, who as a Royalist lord mayor received Charles I there in 1641. It was sequestered in 1644 but restored to Sir George in 1653 and remained in the Whitmore family after the death of Sir George's grandson in 1684. Richard de Beauvoir bought the estate in 1687.

The medieval house was probably swept away by Sir George Whitmore in about 1635, being replaced by a two-storey house of brick, with a steep roof and two levels of dormers. The main front had large pilasters and the house stood in formal gardens, with a line of trees running down to the gatehouse and main entrance to the south. The home farm lay to the south-east. The De Beauvoir family lived at Downham in Essex from the mid-eighteenth century and by 1756 the house was leased to Meyer Schomberg and used as a lunatic asylum. Later resident doctors included John Silvester in 1773, who acquired the former Spurstowe estate near Hackney village. The house later formed part of Thomas Warburton's network of asylums, being used for his rich patients. After the asylum closed in 1851 the house was demolished for the construction of the southern part of De Beauvoir Road and further housing.

Sir John Heron, formerly treasurer of the king's chamber, had used his wealth to acquire an estate round Shacklewell, Kingsland and Newington which he left to his eldest son, Giles, in 1522; his second son was to have the Church Field and a house at Hackney. In 1524 Sir John's widow was the highest assessed for the subsidy. Giles Heron married Cecily, the daughter of Sir Thomas More, but was executed for treason in 1540 and the Shacklewell estate was forfeit. However the house was in the hands of Sir Ralph Sadleir, who may have taken it on to protect it for the family, since two of Giles's sons were described as Sadleir's servants in that year. The house was restored to Giles's eldest son Thomas in 1554 and he sold it to yet another rich London alderman, Thomas Rowe, in 1566.

Rowe had bought his first land in Hackney in 1550 and within seven years had amassed 170 acres. The house at Shacklewell gave him a country seat close to London, where he capped his career as a merchant tailor by becoming lord mayor and being knighted in 1569. Sir Thomas's son, Henry, followed in his father's footsteps with the knighthood and the office of lord mayor. His son, another Henry, succeeded in 1612 and built the Rowe chapel, a family mausoleum in Hackney churchyard. Colonel Owen Rowe, a regicide who died in 1661 and who was also a Hackney resident, may have been a relative. After Sir Henry's death in 1661, his grandson had the property for a mere nine years before his son, the last Henry Rowe, inherited. In 1685 this Henry Rowe sold off the majority of the freehold estate, much encumbered with debt charges, to Francis Tyssen. Even the family pew had gone by 1690 and sixteen years later Henry Rowe returned to Hackney as a pauper seeking parish relief, which he received until 1711. It had taken just over 150 years for the Rowes to rise to riches and crash to the bottom of the social scale.

Sir John Heron's house stood on the north-west side of Shacklewell and was of three storeys, built of brick with the addition of tall sash windows and the Rowe coat of arms in

Sir Henry Rowe (d. 1612), *c.* 1600.

Church Street, looking north across Hackney Brook. This watercolour by Samuel Prout of 1800 shows the scene as it would have appeared in the 1740s.

the glass. It had twenty-five hearths in 1664 and through its occupation by the first two Tyssens from the 1680s to 1717 came to be called the Manor House. It had gone by 1762, replaced by twelve new houses. One of these took over the title of 'Manor House'. Alterations to the rear and refronting after 1820 gave it something of the look of a smaller version of the Church Street Manor House. It was demolished for the construction of Seal Street in the 1880s.

Hackney village centred round the church, built above the confluence of Hackney and Pigwell brooks on ground high enough to avoid flooding. No records survive of any church before 1275. By the end of the thirteenth century the early church had been rebuilt or replaced, with the cost of the building work probably met by the Knights Templars. The dedication from the fourteenth to the mid-seventeenth century was to St Augustine, Bishop of Hippo, also a saint favoured by the Templars order, who drew on his writings. When the Templars order was dissolved in 1324, the Hospitallers took on their estates but the dedication of the church did not change until after 1660, after which variants of St John of Jerusalem, St John the Baptist or the form that became most common, St John at Hackney, were all recorded.

The church manor of Grumbolds and the rectory have been described above. The vicar also had his own house, built as a result of a gift by William de Langford in 1345. This vicarage stood just to the north of the tower of the church, projecting out into the roadway, and may have kept the vicar rather too close to his parishioners for comfort.

No views that show the medieval church survive but the wills of local people provide some details of how it was used and furnished. The late thirteenth-century tower and small chancel would have had several small side chapels, dedicated to different saints. The most important of these was on the south side, dedicated to the Virgin Mary. The cost of lighting the altar was provided from several bequests, including one to 'the Blessed Mary of Humberton'. Medieval Hackney had its own wards and special guilds or fraternities were linked to Church Street (from

1428) and Homerton (from 1451). A guild of the Holy Trinity and the Virgin Mary, founded before 1453, was re-established by the rector and Simon and John Elrington in 1478. This guild, funded by a bequest of property in the City of London, maintained its own brotherhood priest and an assistant at the time of the Dissolution in 1536. Bequests may have funded the construction of the large cross that stood in the nave or one of the aisles before 1454, when a donor left money for a large glass window to illuminate the south wall. The guilds had their own statues, which in 1439 included representations of the Holy Trinity, the Virgin Mary and St Lucy.

Medieval rectors were often pluralists, as the living was often used to supplement the income of royal officials, many of whom were drawn from the clergy in medieval times; for example, Robert de Wadham, rector in 1317, became a Baron of the Exchequer. Hackney's most notable rector was Christopher Urswick, who held the position from 1502 to 1521. Urswick had been instrumental in arranging the marriage of Henry VII to Elizabeth of York and conducted a number of embassies abroad. He was also Dean of York and later Archdeacon of Oxford but settled in Hackney when his diplomatic career ended. Instead he channelled his considerable energies into parish affairs. In conjunction with Sir John Heron (d. 1521), Master of the King's Jewels, Urswick embarked on a major rebuilding of the church. The nave was enlarged at the eastern end and the chancel rebuilt. Heron ensured that his part of the work would be remembered, as the masons carved a number of copies of his coat of arms, with the punning device of the crane, on the walls of the south arcade.

Urswick also built a house in front of the church tower where he lived until his death in 1522, and which later came into parish ownership. Urswick may have been the first burial in the new church; he was buried on the north side of the high altar in a sepulchre topped with a brass of the dean in full clerical vestments. Urswick's tomb survived to be removed from the old to the new church in the 1790s, unlike many other features of the medieval church which were destroyed at the Reformation. The guilds and charities were dissolved, along with the order of the Hospitallers. Images would have been removed and any wall paintings covered or destroyed. The church had an organ in 1500, which is also likely to have been removed. The rectory manor passed into lay hands but the laity made its presence felt within the church. There would have been few seats in the pre-Reformation church but from the 1540s pews gradually began to appear, some attached to individual houses or families. These could be reassigned and also bought or sold. Hackney's sixteenth-century popularity with courtiers and London merchants alike ended up packing the church with pews and additional galleries. Such was the pressure on space that later pews were built over memorials and tombs on the church floor.

No major building changes took place for a century after Urswick's death. In 1606 there was some work on the bells, and the church acquired a clock, but the vestry felt that the carpenter who had acted as the main contractor paid too much for materials and labour and censured 'his excessive expences in drinckinge when he went to gather . . . money'. In 1614 the Rowe family built themselves a mausoleum on the south side of the chancel, later known as the Rowe chapel, though it was never used for worship.

Later vicars were more distinguished than their medieval predecessors. David Doulben, vicar from 1619, became Bishop of Bangor, though he remained a Hackney resident and was buried there in 1633. His successor Gilbert Sheldon went on to become Archbishop of Canterbury and is still commemorated in the Sheldonian Theatre in Oxford. Vicars continued to have assistants after the Reformation and the Puritan thirst for the spoken word led to the appointment of lecturers to preach a Sunday afternoon sermon. Lecturers often doubled up as the parish schoolmaster until the two posts were firmly separated in 1689. In the period of the English Civil War after 1642, Hackney was firmly in the area of Parliamentary control and both its vicars, Calibute Downing and William Spurstowe, were Parliamentarians. Spurstowe was ejected in 1662 but continued to live in his house near the Hackney Brook and became an important focus for many ministers who were to become nonconformists.

By contrast there were few Catholics in Hackney. William Lord Vaux, who had harboured the Jesuit Edmund Campion, rented a house from Lord Mordaunt from 1583 to 1590 and one of his guests there was the conspirator Antony Babington in 1585. Sir Rhys Griffin was a recusant in 1609, as was Isabel Oliver the following year, but in 1619 Richard Abington and his wife were 'late of Hackney' when they were recorded.

Hackney village already had cottages near the rectory house in 1486. Further south there may have been a settlement on the boundary at Cambridge Heath in early medieval times; certainly by 1593 Mare Street was a distinct settlement, which may have included three timber-framed inns, known later as the Nag's Head, the Horse and Groom and the Flying Horse. Shacklewell and its spring had attracted London merchants by the fifteenth century, though it is unlikely that there would have been many houses there other than the Herons' house before the mid-sixteenth century. Clapton would have been similarly sparsely populated but Homerton was the most populous of the parish's divisions in 1605, and had attracted rich Londoners by the 1550s. Sites on the south side of the road at the west end included the Tan House before 1499. Next door Ralph Sadleir had his 'bryk place' built in 1535–6, which was to become today's Sutton House.

Sadleir's father had been a friend of Thomas Cromwell and the young Ralph was in Cromwell's service in 1521 when his father bought the Tan House and land adjoining. Ralph found his future wife in Cromwell's household and from 1535 was in Henry VIII's direct service. The funds from this source enabled him to build an 'H' plan house, with two wings separated by a central range. The curious angle of the wings in relation to the main building reflects the cramped site and the alignment of adjoining buildings. The front of the house was decorated with diapered or overfired bricks to give a lozenge and diamond pattern, while the original windows would all have been at head height on the ground level to give some protection against potential thieves. Rooms included a great hall, with a dais at the west end for a high table, and the panelled great chamber directly above. Beyond it was the main bedchamber with its own privy. The top floor would have been for servants and children. Sadleir sold his house in 1550 to a wealthy wool merchant, John Machell, who was to become Sheriff of London. The Machell family still

Matthias L'Obel at the age of 76. Engraving from a drawing of 1615.

owned it at the end of the sixteenth century, when their neighbour in the Tan House was Thomas Sutton, who moved to Hackney from Stoke Newington after the death of his wife in 1605: he was never resident in Sadleir's house. Later residents of the 'bryk place' included Sir Julius Caesar, Master of the Rolls under James I. Sutton House was to serve as a private school and received its partial Georgian front in 1741–3. It was divided into two in about 1751 and was not brought together until the parish purchased it to serve as St John's church institute in 1890.

Other sixteenth-century residents included Edward, Lord Zouche, whose house may have been opposite Sutton House. Zouche's grounds included a physic garden and he employed Matthias L'Obel as his gardener. The herbalist John Gerard, who visited Hackney and praised the small turnips grown for sale in London, also obtained foreign seeds from Zouche's garden. Zouche was not in continuous residence and there were others who spent time away from Hackney in other houses, including Lord Rich, later Earl of Warwick and Lord Cromwell (d. 1607).

At least the location is known of two other large Homerton houses that vanished. Facing Bridge Street on the north side of Homerton High Street was an imposing two-storey timber-framed range, occupying all the land between Plough Lane (now Furrow Lane) and John (later Bannister) Street. This is likely to have been the country seat of either a London merchant or a royal servant but was later subdivided and demolished in stages from the 1860s, though most of the building was still intact in the late 1870s. The last part went in 1887. Tower Place, at the eastern end of the High Street, dated from the seventeenth century, although its extensive moat suggested that it had replaced a medieval house on or near the same site.

Hackney's first hospital was a medieval foundation. Leprosy was a greatly feared disease across Europe in the twelfth and thirteenth centuries. In England it was decreed in 1200 that lepers could not be housed near the healthy but could live by themselves, building their own church with a churchyard, have a priest of their own and pay no tithes. London had ten leper hospitals on its outskirts, forming a ring round the city, including the Lock Hospital at Kingsland. This had been founded in about 1280 at the southern end of the hamlet of Kingsland, just off Ermine Street, right on the border with Islington parish and had its own chapel. The hospital had its own warden and was supported by rent charges on city property. In 1549 it passed to St Bartholomew's Hospital and became one of its four outhouses. There were substantial repairs in 1605 and the addition of a 'sweatlie ward' in 1613. The Great Fire of London in 1666 depleted the revenues of St Bartholomew's Hospital and resulted in the discharge of all patients but by 1680 Kingsland had twenty patients.

The chapel had been opened to all worshippers as a convenient chapel of ease, though the patients were curtained from the rest of the congregation. The last recorded case of leprosy in London had been in 1557 and by the 1720s patients were suffering from ague, fever, dropsy, jaundice and diarrhoea. Sufferers from venereal disease were also sent there in the mid-1750s. By 1721 successive road repairs had raised Kingsland Road three feet above the hospital, so that the ground-floor wards were very damp. The rebuilding provided for thirty beds, a bagnio, a couch room and a surgery. However the continuing cost of the outstation was eventually to prove too much for the governors of St Bartholomew's Hospital and it was closed in 1760. The tiny chapel, by then dedicated to St Bartholomew, measuring only twenty-seven feet by eighteen feet and twenty feet high, was retained as a chapel of ease. The floor level had not been raised nor had it been rebuilt and in its medieval form it survived until 1846 when it, and the rebuilt hospital building, which had been used for a variety of commercial purposes, were both demolished. The chapel dedication was to be re-used for one of Hackney's new Anglican churches.

3. FROM RESTORATION TO REFORM, 1660–1832

The upheavals of the English Civil War eclipsed the influence of the court on London for the best part of twenty years. Hackney had been a fashionable place to have a country residence for both courtier and wealthy citizen in the sixteenth century but it is likely that the court element was already in decline in the opening years of the seventeenth century. It was to be the city merchants that took their place and bought new estates in the area during the Commonwealth period of the 1650s, so that Hackney and its affairs were to be dominated for the next 170 years by families whose wealth had originally come from their city activities in trade or finance. Defoe thought that there were more than a hundred coaches in Hackney in the 1720s, while in 1756 Hackney was declared to excel all other villages in the kingdom for the opulence of its inhabitants. The wealthy included many of Huguenot descent and there was a small but affluent Sephardic Jewish community, whose first recorded member, Isaac Alvares, a jeweller, bought a house in Homerton in 1674.

Among this wealthy band was the philanthropist Sir John Cass (d. 1718), though he was little-liked in the parish according to Hackney's vicar Peter Newcome. The principal founder of the new East India Company and reputedly England's wealthiest commoner was Sir Gilbert Heathcote (d. 1733) who was also a resident. John Castaing, a banker, had built a large house on the north-west corner of Church Street in 1697, which his daughter sold to John Ward the speculator in 1706. After the collapse of his fortunes in the 1720s Ward may have returned to Hackney and could have been the John Ward of Mare Street who was in receipt of annual bounty money from 1732 to 1750. Another London merchant who owned property in Hackney was Sir Thomas Cooke. On his death in 1695, his Hackney estates were broken up and a substantial part was eventually purchased by Joseph Brooksbank, who was a Hackney resident in 1712. After his death in 1726 his son Stamp Brooksbank commissioned a large house from architect Colen Campbell, approached from a drive on the line of the present Tresham Walk, and standing back from the site of an older house (possibly Cooke's mansion, which was still standing in 1699), which became the site of the stable yards. Hackney House had its own estate of around 122 acres and was set in formal gardens, with two ponds of about 100 feet in diameter with an underground pumping system. Hackney House was sold to John Hopkins after Brooksbank's death in 1756 but survived as a single estate until 1772. Hackney House became a college in 1786 and the remainder of the estate was divided up, some acquired by the owners of 'the Five Houses', which stood between the estate lands and Lower Clapton Road.

The family that became the largest of the new landowners were the Tyssens. Francis Tyssen the elder had married in London in 1649. The previous chapter showed how they came into

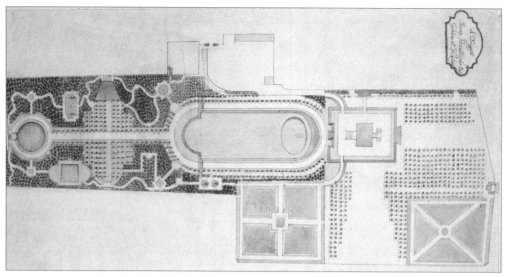

Garden plan of Hackney House probably dating to after 1732 when the house had been completed.

three of the Hackney manors by 1697. The purchase of the Brooke House estate from the Grenville family in 1819 further added to their holdings. The first Francis Tyssen died in 1699 and was succeeded by his son, whose ostentatious funeral in 1710 attracted considerable social comment. His lands and estate, including thirty-two acres in Leyton, were left to another son, Francis III, who married a daughter of Richard de Beauvoir, the owner of the Balmes estate. Francis III died young in 1717, leaving a posthumous son, Francis John Tyssen, who died without legitimate heirs in 1781. His son Francis was left the bulk of the Hackney estate in trust but both he and his brother, Francis John Tyssen, died without heirs in 1813 and 1814 respectively. A daughter, Mary Tyssen, who died in 1800, had married a John Amhurst of Kent and her daughter married William George Daniel of Dorset in 1814. Daniel took the surname Daniel-Tyssen on inheriting.

W.G. Daniel-Tyssen died in 1838 and was succeeded by his son William George Tyssen Daniel-Tyssen who took the surname Tyssen-Amhurst in 1852 and died in 1885. His son William Amhurst Tyssen-Amhurst changed the spelling of his surname to Amherst in 1877 to emphasize a link to a titled family, and became Baron Amherst of Hackney in 1892. Lord Amherst, who was a noted book collector and resident at Didlington Hall, Norfolk, left the bulk of the estate management to the Chestons. Charles Cheston, steward of the manors and the family solicitor, defrauded the estate of considerable income and when his theft came to light after his death in 1906, considerable parts of the Hackney lands had to be sold. However some Hackney property was still owned by the estate as late as 1988 and the family still retain the title of lords of the manor.

Three of Francis III's brothers, including John who lived at Shacklewell and Samuel, were buried at Hackney. One of Francis John's illegitimate sons, Samuel, also a collector, acquired land at Homerton through marriage with Sarah Boddicott, granddaughter of the earlier Samuel, who lived in Norfolk. This branch of the Tyssens held land near Clapton Common, part of which was sold in 1847 to enlarge the holdings of the Craven family.

Clapton House front view, lithograph of about 1840.

Clapton House, which stood just to the north of Clapton Pond on the east side of Lower Clapton Road, was also part of another Hackney estate. This had been put together in the mid-seventeenth century by Thomas Wood, Serjeant of the Pantry, who was a Hackney resident in 1597. He and his eldest son, Sir Henry Wood (d. 1671), who was treasurer to Queen Henrietta Maria and a baronet, both lived at a house on the site. Sir Henry's heir was his brother Thomas, the Bishop of Lichfield and Coventry, on whose death in 1692 the bulk of his estate passed to his nephew Henry Webb. In 1720 the estate was divided among a number of co-heirs, later reunited by the husband of one of the heiresses, Sir William Chapman. Chapman was a casualty of the bursting of the South Sea Bubble and sold the house to a Huguenot silk merchant, Rene de Boyville, in 1723. After de Boyville's death in 1749, his widow sold it to a gem merchant, Jacob de Moses Franco, whose descendants eventually sold the house and twenty-two acres to James Powell.

The Wood house had fourteen hearths in 1672 and may have been built by the bishop's father. Known variously as the Bishop's Mansion, Lizhards or Leezhards, and by 1799 Clapton House, it was virtually rebuilt in 1779–80 for the lessee Israel Levin Salomons, who also built a *yesheva* or private synagogue in the grounds: the first purpose-built place of Jewish worship in Hackney. After Salomons' death in 1788 later tenants converted it into an orangery. By the late eighteenth century the house included a paved marble hall, a library and five acres of pleasure grounds. The Powells never lived there and it ended its days as a private school before being demolished in 1885.

An earlier James Powell was a vintner, who had held land in Hackney in 1718 and one of whose sons features as a rival in love of the diarist Dudley Ryder. But it was a later Powell wine merchant, another James, who built up substantial Hackney landholdings between 1785 and 1821, with purchases from the Tyssens, the heirs of Benjamin Newcome and the Earl of Warwick. James also inherited land in Suffolk from his brother Baden and bought Newick Park in East Sussex. A daughter married another Baden-Powell and he was the grandfather of Robert, Baron Baden-Powell, the founder of the Boy Scouts. Baden-Powell's grandfather held land at Stamford Hill but the Scout leader was never a Hackney resident. Baden-Powell senior's

Rear view of Clapton House when in use as a school, *c.* 1840. The former *yesheva* is on the far right.

younger brother, James Powell, a resident of Shore Place in 1839, bought the Whitefriars glassworks and leased Clapton House from his cousin and brother-in-law, the Revd T.B. Powell. Two of his sons also lived there, including James Cotton Powell, the first incumbent of St James church, Clapton. James Powell, the estate owner, died in 1824 and some of his other purchases went to his daughter Anne, who had married Revd Robert Marriot. These included Cromwell Lodge and neighbouring houses on Lower Clapton Road, plus the extensive Noble's nursery on Pond Lane (later Millfields Road) when the estate was sold in 1882.

James Powell lived at Byland House on the west side of the road opposite the pond, and after his death in 1824 it served as a vicarage for the second and third incumbents of St James church, both Powell relatives. It was sold to Hackney Council in 1932. The council also bought the former premises of the British Asylum for Deaf and Dumb Females, which was probably built for James Coram, a timber merchant, and sold by him in 1714 to Markham Eeles, a china merchant. Eeles is likely to have substantially rebuilt it and decorated the entrance gates with a pair of ornamental urns, from which sprang the local sobriquet of Piss Pot Hall. Between Byland House and the asylum stood a pair of early eighteenth-century houses, one of which was home to the Gaviller family for about a hundred years, but after 1912 had been used by the Salvation Army until damaged in a fire in 1927. Despite local protest all were demolished to make way for the first Powell House estate.

London merchant Edward Misselden owned a house and thirty-one acres of land in South Hackney, on the east side of Grove Street, which he sold to Hugh Norris in 1653. Norris came from a Somerset family and his elder brother, who fought on the Royalist side in the Civil War, suffered for his allegiance. But Hugh, who had made his fortune in London and who went on to become an alderman and treasurer of the Levant Company, was a Parliamentarian and had had a

British Asylum for Deaf and Dumb Females, 179 Lower Clapton Road, *c.* 1910.

good war. The house that went with the estate looked like a fantasia on the theme of Nonsuch Palace, which it resembled. Hugh and his children left it unaltered and it was leased to Robert Ainsworth in 1725, but when Hugh's son Henry decided to resume residence in Hackney it was demolished and James Shepherd, a London builder, completed a new plain Georgian house in 1729–30. Norris set out what Shepherd should do in a contract of extraordinary detail. He intended to raise his status in the area, since he also served on the bench as a local and very active magistrate. Henry's heir moved to Essex and, after his father's death in 1762, the house with its well-stocked gardens was let to Paul Ainsinck, a London merchant. However, Norris's grandson, Henry Norris, a Russia merchant who died in 1804, and his son, the future rector of South Hackney, Henry Handley Norris, were also both resident. After the death of the rector's wife in 1854, the house was left empty and was demolished in the early 1860s when the Norris estate was developed.

Sir John Cass owed his Hackney property to inheritance. The bulk of the Cass land had formed part of the holdings of Henry Monger (d. 1669), founder of the almshouses, who in turn had acquired part of it through his marriage to Bridget Swayne. In 1557 the property had passed to Arthur Dericote, a London draper, who died in 1562 and whose brass survives in St John at Hackney church. Dericote's heir sold to Bridget Swayne's father in 1599. Monger's heirs included Joan Martin and two of his maidservants, one of whom, Hester Eames and her husband Thomas Cass, a carpenter, inherited seventy-five acres of land in 1681 from Joan Martin on her death in 1681. John Cass, later knighted, inherited in 1699 and went on to become a Tory MP and a city alderman. His will created the Sir John Cass Foundation and a school in St Botolph's, Aldgate, although his intention to establish another school at Hackney was not fulfilled. When Elizabeth Cass, Sir John's widow, was admitted to the copyhold

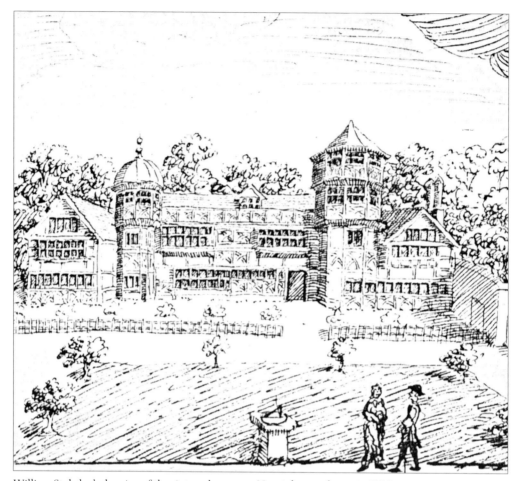

William Stukeley's drawing of the sixteenth-century Norris house, drawn in 1725.

Hackney estate in 1719, it consisted of about eighty-seven acres around Grove Street (the later Lauriston Road) and fifty acres in the marsh. Much of the land was let to successive farmers – Joseph Sureties leased seventy acres stretching from Well Street to Hackney Wick in 1765 as did his successor after 1786, William Gigney.

The earliest record of the estate in 1516 included a cottage at Grove Street. William Leigh, who owned the estate before 1535, had built a house there, which may have passed to Arthur Dericote and in turn could have been one of two houses owned by Monger in 1658. One of these, assessed at sixteen hearths in 1664, was the largest in Grove Street. Monger also leased a house called the George on the west side of the street in 1664 and left another on the east side of the street to Hester Eames in 1669. Cass and his wife leased this house in 1694 and lived in one on the site of the George and this latter house became the Cass family home. There was also a third house in the vicinity. The old Cass house was leased to Henry Norris in 1722, while his own was demolished and a new one built. The house on the east side was home to a Huguenot merchant Peter Thellusson in 1770, while the Cass house was let to the estate surveyor, Jesse Gibson, in 1779. Gibson demolished the old house and replaced it with two new ones, one of which became Grove

Arthur Dericote and family, copied from a brass in St John at Hackney Church.

House School (the name in turn taken from the former Shore Place House and later acquired by Common House at the rear of Monger's almshouses when Grove House school closed).

Sir Francis Bickley, master of the Drapers' Company, served as a member of Hackney's vestry from 1630. He had built up an estate at Dalston, which he sold in 1667 to Sir Stephen White. On his death in 1681 it passed to a namesake and cousin. This grandson sold it in 1753 to James Graham. By 1796 James, son of Sir Robert Graham, a Baron of the Exchequer, held most of the houses that made up Dalston hamlet and a further forty-seven acres. The main house on the estate, which had fifteen hearths when occupied by Bickley in 1664, was later known as Beldames during the White family occupation and was probably the house on the north side of the road opposite the north entrance of the later German Hospital. By 1849 it had been rebuilt and renamed Graham House and survives today as no. 113 Dalston Lane, the headquarters of a housing association. It adjoined the 'Manor House', which may have been the thirteen-hearth house of 1664 occupied by Alderman Thomas Blackall and his wife Mary, whose maiden name became the curious first name of their son, Offspring Blackall (d. 1716), who became Bishop of Exeter. This house was later taken for the Dalston Refuge for Destitute Females.

The Rhodes family were to play a substantial part in the development of Hackney. Thomas Rhodes had the lease of most of Balmes farm by 1773, and his son Samuel Rhodes had acquired ninety-seven acres of the Hackney house estate by 1775. He leased ten acres of Balmes farm to dig brick-earth in 1785 and bought part the former holdings of F. J. Tyssen, east of the Kingsland Road in 1778–9. This included the Lamb Inn and much of London Fields farm, which were later to form the Lamb Farm estate, one of the first large areas of Hackney to be built over in the next century.

Dudley Ryder's grandfather had been the first of the family to live in Hackney. He had been ejected from his living in Warwickshire in 1662 and would have come to Hackney visiting his cousin Robert Billio, after the latter succeeded William Bates as minister to the Hackney congregation in 1699. Dudley's son Richard (d. 1733), who became a partner in a linen draper's business in Cheapside, invested his profits in property in Hackney. In 1704 he bought part of the estate of the late Sir Thomas Cooke, including the later Upton House on the east side of Upper Homerton, and this became the family home to his children, including the diarist

Urswick Road, looking north, with the former Ryder house in use as Upton House industrial school. Photograph Alfred Braddock, 1884.

Dudley Ryder. The Ryders also built a house to the south, opposite the entrance to the later Sutton Place and home of David Powell, elder brother of James, in 1810 and Charles Rivaz and his family from 1847. The Ryders later moved to Church Street, where they acquired much of the former property of the Vyner family, including the Black and White House. In 1733 the Dudley Ryder inheritance included the Plough public house and adjoining land at Homerton. By the end of the century the family owned houses in Ryder Place (later taken for the construction of the North London Railway) and Bohemia Place. The family still owned property in Chalgrove Road in 1931. Upton House, rebuilt in 1776–7, survived as no. 2 Urswick Road until 1885 when the truant school it housed was closed to be rebuilt as a board school.

Isaac Alvares bought a house in Homerton in 1684 which had been owned by Rachel Denham in 1624 and Robert Johnson in 1643. Johnson's property passed to the Carteret family and it was Sir Edward who sold it to Alvares. He and his daughter Deborah lived there but she and her husband David Alvares sold it to George Bonnet in 1698. It passed by inheritance to the Milborne family and is likely to have been the house Hackney parish leased as a workhouse in 1732.

Another Alvares, though not necessarily a relative, Jacob Alvares, was living in Clapton in 1716. In that year his house burned down and he bought an estate between Mare Street and London Fields, where his descendants were to live for a century. He joined a small but established Sephardic Jewish community in that part of Hackney, which included Moses Silva, Jacob Cohen, Gabriel Lopes Pinheiro and Benjamin Mendes de Costa, who moved to Homerton in 1727. Although there is little direct evidence of anti-Semitism in Hackney, it is likely that the frequent nominations of Jews to parochial office was intended to produce payments to be excused office. In one period nine out of thirty-five nominees were Jewish, which would seem to be out of proportion to the community's relative size. There was also a case of the overrating of Jewish property in 1733 when Jacob Alvares, Pinheiro and the da Costas successfully appealed to the magistrates, who included Henry Norris. The wealth of some members of the community was well known and possibly overstated: when Jacob Mendes de Costa died in 1751 he was said to be worth over £70,000 and in 1780 it was claimed that Israel Salomons, who had leased Clapton House, had asked Hackney vestry if they would compensate him if the silver gates he was proposing to put up in front of the house were damaged. In 1760 Benjamin Mendes da Costa and Jacob de Moses Franco were among the first members of the Jewish Board of Deputies in 1760, when every single member of the *Mahammed* had a house in Hackney.

By that time there had been some dispersal of the community from the Mare Street area. The tobacco merchant Joshua Israel Brandon came to Clapton in 1742, though he also owned property in Homerton, including a house still owned by his son Jacob de Fonseca Brandon in 1832, and London Fields, including a nursery south of Exmouth Place. Brandon put considerable outlay into both house and grounds. After his death in 1772 the description of his property included the

> garden of 2 acres, well disposed and laid out in an exact manner with grass plots and serpentine gravel walks, which lead to a canal in which is a great plenty of goldfish; near the canal is erected an elegant Chinese summer house, the most admired in this country, raised on eight moveable columns with Chinese stairs and galleries round the same, four sash windows and a well finished temple on top.

Isaac Alvares did not leave Mare Street as he had conducted considerable building works there. He bought a large house and six other smaller ones in 1730 for his great-grandson, Isaac Jessurun Alvares. Isaac further expanded the holding and built another house alongside, together with a smaller one on his estate for his mistress Mrs Jenkins. The estate was inherited by his son by Mrs Jenkins, George Jenkins, in 1809.

In the later eighteenth century Stamford Hill had a number of notable Jewish residents. The earliest was the Italian-born Moses Vita Montefiore, a resident by 1763. His grandson married Henrietta Rothschild, daughter of the financier Nathan Meyer Rothschild. Rothschild had originally leased one of the Five Houses from Thomas Boddington in 1815 but he only stayed a year and the list of breakages – even the mahogany chairs in the housekeeper's room were listed as 'broke' – in the concluding inventory suggest either a very boisterous family, or a very decrepit house. In 1821 Rothschild leased a house that had been vacated by Joseph Taylor MP that was about thirty years old. It was just north of the Montefiore house on the west side of Stamford Hill near the later Colberg Place. It was the largest in the road, having a substantial carriage sweep at the front, a long wing to the north, two curved bays at the rear and a substantial conservatory on the south side. Nathan's wife Hannah liked Hackney and found 'the situation more agreeable than the streets of London; we do not have any of the benefit from our National friend, the fog'. The Rothschild family left Stanford Hill in 1835 when they bought Gunnersbury House.

Israel Salomons also had links with the Germans' Hambro synagogue and in 1786 a group of Ashkenazim acting for the synagogue bought land on the east side of Grove Street for burials.

This remained in use from 1786 to 1892 when the synagogue closed and the disused burial ground survives on Lauriston Road today, though the eighteenth-century prayer hall appears to have been demolished shortly after the closure of the cemetery.

Some idea of what was on the market comes from an advert for a large house at the edge of London Fields in 1731. The prospective tenant would have entered through a large hall paved with marble. On the ground floor were three parlours, a large smoking room and at the rear a servants' hall, kitchen and other service rooms. Upstairs there were thirteen rooms, each with closets and many with marble chimney pieces 'and very good pictures'. At the rear was a brewhouse, three coach houses, stabling for fifteen horses and a large garden planted with 'wall' and other fruit trees.

Large houses also supported large gardens. John Evelyn visited the Brooke House garden in May 1654, 'one of the neatest and most celebrated in England' and another Hackney garden belonging to Mr Tombs, where he was impressed with the 'large noble walks, some modern statues; but what was prettiest was the Vine-yard planted in Strawberry-borders, staked at ten foote distant'. Samuel Pepys visited Brooke House in June 1664 'and here I first saw oranges grow, some green, some half, some a quarter and some full ripe on the same tree . . . I pulled off a little one by stealth (the man being mighty curious of them) and eat it; and it was just as other green small oranges are; as big as half the end of my little finger. Here were also great variety of other exoticque plants, and several Labrinths and a pretty Aviary.'

Hackney provided a venue for annual meetings of those interested in gardening. In 1749 the annual Florist's Feast was held at the White Horse 'where there were present a great number of

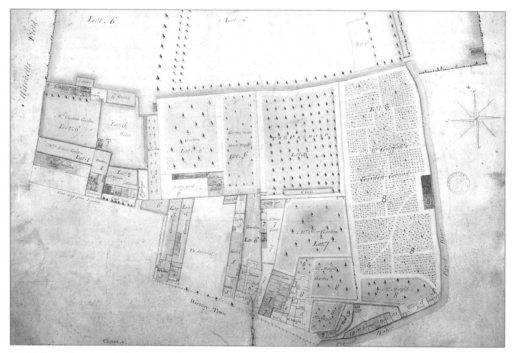

Dr William Spurstowe's former Hackney estate as it appeared just before John Silvester bought it in 1761. It lay on the west side of Church Street. The Spurstowe house is marked just south of Pigwell Water and Mr Griffith's garden ground was later to form part of Silvester's garden. Mr Oliver's house on the street (no. 7) includes a schoolroom and was almost certainly being used as one of Hackney's private schools.

curious Florists, and a prize given to him that produced the best six whole-blowing carnations, which was decided in favour of Mr Montford of Lambeth. The Company made a grand procession thro' the principal Streets of Hackney, the Stewards being adorned with Crowns of Flowers, decorated in a most beautiful Manner, with a Band of Musick attending them, and the whole was conducted with the utmost Decency and Decorum.' These informal meetings ultimately led to the foundation of the Horticultural Society of London in 1804. City livery companies also held herbalizing feasts at Hackney. In 1767 the warden of the Apothecary's Company gave a discourse at Hackney on discovering the genus of various plants, including the white nettle. But well-stocked local gardens were also the target of thieves who stole two pots of double stocks and one of sassafras from the forecourt of Nehemiah Brooke's house in Mare Street in 1754, and in February 1768 robbers removed large quantities of carp and tench from a number of ornamental ponds.

Some of those buying houses in Hackney would have found old-fashioned or run-down gardens and wished to make changes. One such was Dr John Silvester, an army physician of Huguenot descent, who was one of the doctors at Balmes House lunatic asylum by 1773. Silvester had earlier bought the house and estate to the west of Church Street that had once belonged to William Spurstowe. Spurstowe's granddaughter and her husband had sold the estate to a physician, Dr Francis Douce, in 1719. In 1724 the house (roughly on the site of nos 1–19 Amhurst Road) lay just to the south of the Hackney Brook, which had been diverted to create three ornamental canals thirty years previously, later the subject of litigation. The last of the canals ran back into the brook via a necessary house – why waste water? The formal ornamental grounds with the prominent necessary house were not to Silvester's taste and he employed a young German whom he had met in Holland to change them. This was Conrad Lochlies, who came to England in 1761 and later anglicized his name to Loddiges.

Loddiges, born in 1738, was the grandson of a gardener who had served the Electors of Hanover, who were also kings of England from 1714. After an apprenticeship to a court gardener, he had travelled to the Low Countries, possibly with the hope of going on to England. Loddiges was able to introduce foreign shrubs to Silvester's garden, among them the mauve rhododendron, and relandscape the grounds. Silvester sold the estate in 1777, by which time:

In the Gardens, which are delicately laid out, and abound with the best of fruits etc., are two greenhouses, a Fruiting-house and Succession-house. A curious Grotto, with a constant Stream murmering through, replenishing a Canal well-stored with Fish; and at the entrance thereto a Willow of magnitude, with extending branches, affording a refreshing shade. A Farm-yard with Barn, Stable, Cow-

Conrad Loddiges in old age.

house etc. and 15 acres of land in high manurage; running through the centre thereof a brook making five falls, the last in clamourous murmur; a Gothic Hermitage faces this cascade, which may be easily converted into a Cold Bath. A Shrubbery and Serpentine Walk (with flowering shrubs) nearly encompass the whole.

Vandals broke into the empty property in October 1777 and damaged plants and 'a fine Chinese bridge' but by that time Loddiges had left Silvester's employment. In 1769 he had married and early in the following year sought his employer's advice on setting up his own business as a nurseryman. Hackney already had a number of small plant nursery businesses. The earliest Hackney nursery traced to date belonged to James Thynne near London Fields in 1666, but by 1745 nurseries and market gardens lined both sides of Mare Street. Another German immigrant, Johann Busch, who was also from Hanover, had leased a number of small sites around Mare Street in 1756 and through contact with an importer of American seeds, Busch became an important supplier to the German market. Closer to home he also sold unusual plants to Princess Augusta, whose plant collection forms the basis of the Royal Botanic Gardens at Kew.

In 1771 Busch was appointed Imperial Head Gardener and landscape artist to the Russian Empress, Catherine the Great. There his achievements included the remodelling of Tsarkoe Great Park but his departure offered Loddiges his chance. Loddiges' life savings of £100 were insufficient to acquire the whole of Busch's business but he took over the importation of exotic seeds and some of Busch's clients. Busch continued to rent some nursery land in Hackney, one of which was managed for him by Jeremiah Bentham, father of the philosopher Jeremy Bentham. Busch's son Joseph retained land near Graham Road until 1815.

But the future of the Hackney nursery lay with Loddiges. Conrad rented a house on the corner of London Lane and Mare Street in 1775, which served him as a seed shop and home, together with nursery ground nearby. A neighbouring estate owner, W.T. Corbett, recalled seeing old Loddiges wheeling dung through the gate at the London Lane end of his premises, and this must have been in the early days of the shop. Two years later Loddiges published a remarkable trilingual plant catalogue, in English, German and Latin, the first of a distinguished series of printed catalogues from him and his sons. Profits from the business enabled Loddiges to acquire an old house on the east side of Mare Street. This was Barber's Barn, reputed to date from about 1590, and which had been leased to the regicide John Okey in 1658. It had been in use as a private school but now Loddiges demolished it and built a house for himself and the adjoining Loddiges terrace to the south. The land behind, incorporating part of Paradise Field, was laid out as a plant nursery. John Renton, who had owned a Hoxton nursery, served as head gardener and his son was later to paint the family portraits.

Conrad Loddiges contributed to the *Botanical Magazine* and was praised in its pages for his plant introductions. But it was from 1816, with the publication of the *Botanical Cabinet*, with its coloured plates of plants combined with spectacular experimental glasshouses and hothouses, that the nursery made its name. Much of this was owed to George Loddiges, Conrad's son, who introduced steam-heating and a rain sprinkler system that imitated tropical rain. Loddiges' palm house pre-dated the one at Kew by twenty-four years and was described by garden writer John Loudon as 'the largest hothouse in the world'. In the 1830s this Grand Palm House was overcrowded and Joseph Paxton designed another for the nursery, which was the first to use laminated wood for large-scale construction. Both hothouses were precursors of Paxton's work at Chatsworth and his designs for the Crystal Palace built to house the Great Exhibition of 1851.

Loddiges were famous for their orchids. This is
Blaetia Tankerville, introduced by Dr Fothergill in
1778, as depicted in *The Botanical Cabinet*.

Cover for *The Botanical Cabinet* 1826.

But for plant collectors Loddiges was best known as the first firm to commercially cultivate orchids and for many years was the principal English orchid supplier. The grounds also included an arboretum, begun in 1816 and one of the first in Britain. Among the many customers needing trees was the newly created Abney Park Cemetery in the 1830s. If all this was not enough George Loddiges was also a renowned ornithologist and owned a large collection of hummingbirds. Sadly his comparatively early death in 1846 aged sixty, followed by the death of his brother William in 1849, coincided with the development of the Mare Street area for building and the lease on the nursery site was due to expire in 1853. George's son Conrad gradually ran down the business down and sold the stock off. The residue was acquired for the Great Exhibition and the nursery closed in 1852. The buildings were sold in 1854, except for the family home and Loddiges Terrace. The former was demolished in 1899 but the latter survives today.

The wealthy were supported by servants, some of whom would have lived in their employer's homes, and Isaac Alvares employed five servants in his Mare Street house in 1780. Some would have worn full livery. In 1765 Sir Thomas Fludyer's house was broken into and the thief got away with his servant's uniform; 'one livery close bodied blue cloth greatcoat, faced with blue shalloon, a blue cape laced round with a purple, black and white worsted lace, with white metal basket buttons, one pair of boots and boot garters and one light coloured fustian frock with a turn down collar and mohair buttons'. But those aspiring to service had to know their place. In 1778 one young woman seeking employment as a chambermaid arrived at the

George Loddiges.

door of a house in Hackney in a blue satin calash (a dress supported by a framework of whalebone and regarded as an extravagant fashion). Her prospective employer was doubly horrified – by the dress and that the fashion had penetrated to 'the lower orders'. Some local residents had connections with the West Indies, like Richard Gosling, 'a Barbadoes merchant' and a director of the Royal Exchange who died in 1769. There were some black servants in seventeenth and eighteenth-century Hackney. The parish registers record the burial of Antony 'a poore old negro aged 105 years' in 1630. In June 1783 a black servant 'belonging to a gentleman near Kingsland' met two members of the watch on Kingsland Road and, thinking he was about to be attacked, fired a blunderbuss and injured one of them. But black people were comparatively uncommon. In 1737 George Scipio, a chapman of Shoreditch, was accused by Anne Godfrey of stealing her washing. The evidence was flimsy: a black man had been seen in the vicinity at the time of the theft and he was the only black man known to Godfrey. The case got no further than the magistrate.

Eighteenth-century Hackney was home to the rich but it also housed the poor and was easily reached by London criminals. Travellers were at risk on the Hackney Road from highwaymen and the seclusion of the marshes offered smugglers a route into the capital. In July 1721 Hackney's watch stopped a group of men, thinking them housebreakers. Some fast talking ensued and the watch were persuaded otherwise but the men made off rather quickly, leaving behind them 1,000 lb of smuggled tea. Burglary was a common crime. Joseph Sureties lost some household silver in a break-in at his London Fields home in 1771, including spurs, salt cellars and two sets of buckles. Hen houses and duck ponds were being regularly raided in 1751–2; one of the victims was Stephen Ram and another one of his neighbours in Shepherd's Lane, who lost a fine Bengal duck. Dead birds could be sold for 6d in Spitalfields market early in the morning with no questions asked, though even then the amount of money was felt to be very small for the risk involved. There were more serious crimes, including robbery with violence, and in 1763 there was reported the attempted rape of a four-year-old child – the offender was punished with a mere six weeks imprisonment but had to stand in the pillory. At the other end of the scale there were nuisance offences. Justice Henry Norris fined his own coachman for swearing. In 1801 the lock was stolen off the door of St John at Hackney church.

'This is the most impudent robbery that has been committed for some time' commented the newspaper report.

Those criminals who were caught ended up in front of a local justice of the peace. One such was Henry Norris, a merchant and supporter of the Whig government of the 1730s, who saw service on the bench as a way of improving his social standing. Norris kept a notebook for the years 1730–41 of cases he heard at his house in Grove Street. Unique among English counties, Middlesex had no county assizes and all serious cases were referred on to the judges of the King's Bench and Common Pleas. Those apprehended were held in the City of London gaol at Newgate and their cases held at the Middlesex Sessions House, Hicks Hall, Clerkenwell. There were many cases of assault and while the highwayman Dick Turpin, who is reputed to have used a house in Hackney as a hideaway, does not appear, some of his associates in the Gregory gang were active in the area, for example in 1735, when evidence was presented of the involvement of John Jones of Homerton in a number of violent robberies. There was a case of a farmer and his family who were robbed in their own home by a group of soldiers in 1728, identified as such by the cockade left behind after the attack, which the newspaper report suggested they 'ought not to leave . . . behind when they go upon such Expeditions, such things being of no use but upon Reviews'. Gin was the century's equivalent of hard drugs and in 1732 a child of under two was abandoned naked in a necessary house after her mother had pawned its clothes to buy drink.

The penalties for conviction were high. Theft from a dwelling house of 40s or more or theft from a person of 1s would lead to hanging. Some offenders escaped death by juries downvaluing goods, so that the lesser penalty of transportation resulted. Sometimes juries refused to convict at all, though one juryman robbed near the Shoulder of Mutton (London Fields) in 1752 had

The Cat and Mutton alehouse on the south-west corner of London Fields. From a wash drawing by C. Bigot of about 1830.

little thanks from one of his assailants, whom he had had a hand in letting off although he and his fellows believed him guilty. His appeal for his watch and pocket book were to no avail: 'Curse your eyes, you son of a B—ch, learn to do justice another time' was the thief's reply, before making off with his companion across the fields – with the stolen goods.

Hackney vestry offered regular rewards for information leading to conviction of criminals from the 1740s onwards. They also prosecuted in cases that directly concerned them, as in 1756, when Mary Tull locked up a servant girl in an outhouse for several days without food, with a dead body for company, and then had a servant dump her unconscious body at Stamford Hill. Although the vestrymen were horrified at this act of barbarity, they would also have been concerned that they would become financially responsible for the servant, who was nursed back to health in the workhouse but ultimately sent out of the parish. Improvements to the watch and to lighting on the turnpike roads did lead to a drop in the crime rates (to the point where in 1772 it was claimed there had not been a single robbery on the Hackney Road for several weeks). In 1829 the vestry objected strongly to Hackney's inclusion in the Metropolitan Police area, claiming that the new police would not provide adequate protection or maintain night patrols, and that the locally employed parish watchmen, who knew the area, would be thrown out of work. However the petition failed and a police station was set up next to the old church tower, joined by another on Kingsland High Street just south of Shacklewell Lane by 1842.

Hackney had no local press of its own but features in national newspapers and periodicals give some sense of what constituted the good stories of the day. Floods could cause problems at Hackney, as in April 1756 when spring rains made it dangerous for horses and carriages to cross the brook. Reckless driving was the cause of an accident in April 1762 when a servant on horseback was trapped between two post-chaises near Hackney village racing to get to London. One chaise overturned on top of him, crushing his leg; it was righted and both drivers made off, leaving him critically injured and his horse dead. There were regular incidents of carters not riding properly on their vehicles and trouble with the precursors of the London cabbie. Stage coachmen plied for hire by St John at Hackney church. In September 1751 two were fined for refusing to take a fare to Bishopsgate station, despite the gentlemen offering them 3s for a 2s fare. Rather than this being the eighteenth-century equivalent of 'not going south of the river at this time of night' it seems to have become local practice to charge excessive fares for Sunday travel.

Local accidents and scandal also made the news. In January 1765 a farmer was killed by his pet monkey, who managed to fire a fowling piece into the body of his sleeping owner. Henry Fielding's fictional Squire Allworthy, who features in his novel *Tom Jones*, published in 1749, had an unfortunate Clapton antecedent. The Hackney Allworthy, a local JP, had a daughter, Susanna, whose roving eye in church was noticed by Dudley Ryder in March 1716. At a bonfire to celebrate the accession of George II outside Allworthy's house in August of the same year, Ryder noticed her deep in conversation with her brother-in-law, the son of the wealthy Sir Gilbert Heathcote. Four years later Heathcote junior seduced Susanna and carried her off with the help of her maid, Anne Fletcher. The newspapers carried reports of the trial of Heathcote and Fletcher for abduction in July 1720; both were found guilty and the unfortunate Susanna died in childbirth the following year.

Like any community, eighteenth-century Hackney had its prostitutes, though there are few records of their presence. Dudley Ryder records a number of assignations in or near the City of London including one in April 1716, when he came home after midnight 'very warm with drinking wine and had a mighty inclination to fill a whore's commodity', though when he was accosted by one he was 'confounded what to say to her and could not rally her as I would have done, so after some little discourse, I parted with her and came home'.

It was a different kind of health issue that angered some of the inhabitants of Church and Mare Streets. In February 1768 Dr Thomas Ruston rented a house in Mare Street to inoculate healthy people against smallpox, intending to open it in the following month. There were complaints to the vestry and although Ruston tried to stand firm, his windows were smashed in March and by April he moved elsewhere. Mental illness, not being potentially infectious, caused fewer problems. Besides Brooke House and Balmes House, the Black and White House was used for the insane in 1724, while Pembroke House on Mare Street housed lunatic employees of the East India Company from 1818 to its closure for demolition in 1870. London House, nearby, was also an asylum from about 1826 until the mid-1860s, while Leny Smith's house on the present Kenworthy Road (now the Convent of the Sacred Heart) was used by Dr Tuke to provide a rather better class of care for wealthy patients in 1831.

As Hackney's population grew the capacity of the parish church became even more stretched. Major repairs were undertaken in 1756 and 1779 and piecemeal additions had raised capacity to 1,000 people. Though the church was not rebuilt, when Peter Newcome became the vicar in 1704 he determined that he could not live in the old vicarage. Its six rooms and attached brewhouse were 'ready to fall down and irreparable'. After solemn inspection by a posse of local clerics, who included the parish lecturer and antiquarian John Strype, Newcome got his way. The old vicarage was demolished (the cross next to the Midland Bank marks the site) and a new one built by subscription, roughly on the site of the modern vicarage, which was to survive, with alterations in 1829, until after the Second World War.

Rams Episcopal Chapel, Homerton High Street. View looking east, 1740.

The east end of the old St John at Hackney Church and the houses facing the churchyard. From a painting by John Varley dating to shortly before demolition began in 1797.

Besides St Bartholomew's chapel, the parish had two proprietary chapels. The wealthy Irishman Stephen Ram had bought a house and land on the north side of Homerton High Street in 1723. When he was unable to secure a pew in St John's church, he built his own chapel in his garden in 1723, which remained family-owned until 1791. Use of lay preachers led it to be described as Methodist in 1795 but it remained Low Church Anglican and had a congregation of 400 in 1851. The chapel looked like a small brewery with a pepper-pot tower and was demolished after closure in 1935.

The present St Thomas church at Clapton also began as a proprietary chapel, built by John Devall in about 1774 for the tenants of his new houses. For many years it was served by the assistant curate at Hackney, Revd Jellinger Symons (d. 1810), and it had various owners until it was sold to Joshua Watson, brother of the vicar of St John's in 1827.

Hackney churchyard was enlarged in 1763 and finally the lack of seats in the church compelled the parish to take action. An act of Parliament created trustees to manage the building of a new church to the north of the old one in Church Field. The body of the old church was demolished in 1797, along with Urswick's House, leaving only the tower standing. A new church, designed by James Spiller, was completed in July 1797, though the tower was outside the parochial budget and was not added until 1814. An active member of the trustees had been the young James Watson and when the old vicar, Thomas Cornthwaite, who had been in post since 1753 and in latter years was often absent due to sickness, finally died in 1799, Watson became the vicar. Watson and his brother Joshua, together with others including his curate and South Hackney landowner Henry Handley Norris, constituted the group known as the Hackney Phalanx. The Phalanx was highly influential in national Anglican affairs for the next twenty or so years. One of Joshua Watson's college friends became the Tory Prime Minister, Lord Liverpool, and Norris exerted considerable influence on national church appointments. Joshua Watson retired from his wine merchant's business in 1811 and took a house on Lower Clapton Road, just north of Clapton Passage. He was a regular workhouse visitor and worked with his brother on a Hackney programme of church building and school formation. Norris was the principal founder of the Society for Promoting Christian Knowledge and came to be squire and parson of South Hackney. Working with the Watsons he helped fund a chapel of ease for South Hackney on the north side of Well street, which was completed in 1810

Henry Handley Norris, squire and parson of South Hackney, *c.* 1820. (Engraving published 1842.)

and served the district until superseded by the present St John of Jerusalem church in 1848. The chapel building was demolished but the graveyard, full of tombs of local people including the Frampton family, remains in front of St Thomas Place.

In 1825 the parish was divided into three, with St John's chapel in South Hackney becoming a parish church, and a new church built on Stoke Newington Road. This was West Hackney church, completed in 1825 and designed by Robert Smirke. Norris and the Watsons were still concerned about the pressure on existing Anglican churches and in 1839 formed a committee to channel into new buildings, though, sadly, J.J. Watson died before the committee began to implement its proposals.

Hackney played an important part in the history of nonconformity in the London area. A travelling preacher, John Davenport, was reported to be in the area in 1637 and there were signs of radical religious movements emerging during the English Civil War, when a group calling themselves the Re-Baptists gathered on the banks of the River Lea for mutual immersion in 1641, some going in on horseback. In the Commonwealth period Mrs Salmon, a Presbyterian, and Hannah Woolley, a Puritan, both ran schools in the parish. But after his ejection former Hackney vicar William Spurstowe provided a focus for many like-minded colleagues and Puritan London merchant families could offer patronage and financial support. Friends meetings took place in secret in Hackney in 1662 and in 1665 twenty-five people were reported for attending a conventicle in Margaret Hammond's house, including the merchant Thomas Barnardiston.

Homerton Academy, an engraving by George Hawkins made
in September 1823, shortly after the old house
was demolished to be replaced by a new college building.

A 'lecture by combination' was reported in 1669, involving such well-known preachers as Philip Nye, William Bates and Peter Sterry, who had been chaplain to Oliver Cromwell. The Declaration of Indulgence allowed the establishment of an enduring weekly lecture based in London and for meeting houses to be licensed. Ten houses in Hackney were so licensed, including the house of London alderman John Forth and of four ejected ministers. Rich residents like Sir Thomas Vyner, Sir Stephen White, Thomas Cooke and Nathaniel Barnardiston were all Anglicans but left evidence in their wills of their support for nonconformist ministers like Bates.

Hackney's many private schools continued to include some run by dissenters. George Fox, the founder of the Society of Friends, visited one at Shacklewell in 1671 and again in 1684 when it was run by Jane Bullock. Martin Morland probably taught at Hackney, a connection that was to lead to his son Benjamin founding a long-lived school. Sir Thomas Marsh was also reported to have used his house as an academy for training nonconformist ministers in 1682.

Marsh's Academy was the precursor of a number of institutions intended to train ministers. The King's Head Academy was founded at Plasterers Hall in London but moved in 1768 to an old house on the north side of Homerton High Street. From 1800 the principal tutor was John Pye Smith and the King's Head Society passed over control of the academy to the Homerton Academy Society in 1817, by which time it accommodated masters, students and a large library. The old building had been enlarged in 1811 but was rebuilt to the design of architect Samuel Robinson in 1823, and in the same year the name was changed to Homerton College. Graduates could qualify for degrees from London University from 1840 and after amalgamation with Highbury and Coward Colleges became part of New College in 1852. The Homerton premises were used solely for teacher training and were transferred to the

Joseph Priestley, from an engraving published in 1795.

St Thomas Square Chapel, drawn by W. Hammon, *c.* 1841.

control of the Congregational Board of Education. The changing social condition of Homerton in the 1880s, combined with student deaths from typhoid, prompted a move and the college relocated to Cambridge in 1892, retaining the Homerton name.

The history of Congregational institutions in Hoxton was covered in the first volume in this series, *More Light, More Power*. When the Hoxton Square Academy closed, a number of eminent local dissenters, including Richard Price of the Old Gravel Pit chapel, acquired the empty Hackney House in 1786 and added two wings to take up to seventy-five students. Teachers included the radical Gilbert Wakefield and the scientist, philosopher and minister Joseph Priestley, while students included the literary critic William Hazlitt. In the atmosphere of the reaction to the French Revolution, the concentration of so many extremists and the political radicalism of the curriculum alarmed the government, who spied on the college. Student indiscipline contributed to the undermining of public support and financial problems led to its closure in 1796, after which the house was demolished and the estate divided. Thomas Belsham, who succeeded Priestley after the latter left for America, and who had also been a tutor at the college, took pupils into his own house in Grove Place after 1796. College House, built on the foundations of Cooke's old house for one of the resident tutors, Abraham Rees, lasted as a private residence until about 1883.

The Hackney Theological Seminary, initially called the Hackney Academy and after 1871 Hackney College, was not the radical institution its predecessor had been. It was founded in 1803 as a result of a donation by Homerton resident Charles Townsend and took up the work proposed by John Eyre for educating ministers that he had outlined in his Village Itinerancy or Evangelical Association for the Propagation of the Gospel. One of the managers was George Collison, a Walthamstow minister, who also served as one of the tutors. The seminary took over Eyre's former house on the south side of Well Street near the junction with Grove Street (later Lauriston Road), with students living in converted stables at the rear until a new college was built on the site in 1843. Training Congregational ministers became the main work of the college, which moved to Finchley in 1887, and the building was taken over as a workhouse.

Hackney's oldest meeting house originated in the preaching of Philip Nye and William Bates in the 1660s and was first registered in 1694. It was converted from former houses and stood on the west side of Mare Street. There were fewer than 100 communicants in 1712. The election of John

Robert Aspland.

Barker in 1714 led to a breakaway group founding a chapel on a former gravel pit field near Mare Street's bowling green opposite St Thomas Square. The original meeting house moved to a new building on the Mare Street just south of St Thomas Square in 1773, under the auspices of their minister Samuel Palmer. That church was enlarged in 1824 and had schoolrooms added in 1841. Palmer's successor was Henry Forster Burder. The church was conveyed to the Presbyterians in 1896 and ceased to be a place of worship in 1912.

In 1715 the Old Gravel Pit worshippers moved to a new chapel south of Morning Lane and east of the future Chatham Place: this was enlarged in 1787. Under the ministry of Richard Price the church became Unitarian in doctrine, a trend confirmed by Price's successors Priestley and Belsham, though only formally stated after the church moved to a new rotunda-like building further south on Chatham Place in 1809, which became the New Gravel Pit chapel. The old church had been considered unsafe after an elderly member of the congregation fell asleep during a service and leaned against one of the iron pillars supposedly supporting the roof – which moved. But the building was to see further religious service, for it was leased to the Congregationalists who had formed a church associated with John Pye Smith's new academy in 1804.

The new Unitarian congregation under the minister Robert Aspland soon found their new building required repair and had to worship in the Mermaid Inn while work was put in hand in 1824. A new building in the Gothic style was put up in 1858 but this coincided with the long decline of the congregation from the later nineteenth century onwards, though the church did not finally close until 1969.

The Old Gravel Pit chapel was enlarged in 1853 and may have received a pedimented front at the same time. The congregation moved to the imposing Clapton Park chapel in 1871 but the old building was still used as a Sunday school for two years, before becoming an undenominational mission. It survived in industrial use, much altered, and today has a plaque on the north wall facing Morning Lane which commemorates the ministry of Joseph Priestley.

There was also a Congregational chapel at Kingsland, founded in 1789 and arising from prayer meetings held by Thomas Cranfield for local bricklayers at the foreman's house. Summer evening services were also held on Kingsland Green. A permanent chapel was built in Robinson's Row on the west side of Kingsland High Street in 1792, and enlarged in 1840 and 1845. A new chapel on Sandringham Road was opened in 1852, which lasted until shortly before 1951. There was also a small chapel associated with the Hackney Theological Seminary, which had its own building in the angle between Grove Street and Hackney Terrace (Cassland Road). This opened in 1805 and ceased to be used for worship in 1847 when the Hampden chapel in Lauriston Road opened. It was demolished before 1870.

The New Gravel Pit chapel of 1809, and its replacement of 1858.

The first Baptist congregation in Hackney worshipped in a small house in Shore Place in 1796. A chapel was also built there but was eventually replaced by a new church on the west side of Mare Street, north of the Flying Horse public house, in 1812. Ministers included F.A. Cox, one of the founders of both the Baptist magazine and London University. The Mare Street chapel was destroyed by fire in 1854 and replaced by a grander building designed by W.G. and E. Habershon, completed in 1856. This church was bomb-damaged in 1940 and virtually destroyed by a V2 rocket in 1945, after which a new church was created in Frampton Park Road. There was also a small chapel in Homerton Row, founded by Thomas Eason, and which opened another small chapel on the south side of the road in 1822; this was in existence until the early 1960s.

Radicalism in religion went with radicalism in politics. Freeholders shared in the election of two members of parliament for Middlesex. John Wilkes was eventually elected after attempts by the court to block the election result of 1768. Political meetings at the Mermaid assembly rooms were attended by Wilkes and other Whig politicians of the day, including Charles James Fox. The French Revolution of 1789 caused considerable excitement on this side of the channel and branches of radical clubs were established in Hackney. In 1793 the London Corresponding Society held an open-air demonstration, probably on Hackney Downs. A broadsheet supporting the views of Tom Paine, author of *The Rights of Man*, was published from Shacklewell by the Society for the Friends of Liberty in 1796. But there was also considerable fear of potential revolution, especially after England went to war with France in 1793. The Hackney Association for the Preservation of Peace, Liberty and Property first met in December 1792, drawing support from landowners like Powell, Graham, Norris and Rhodes, and supported by the vicar,

A Hackney Volunteer, as drawn by Rowlandson in 1798. The uniform consisted of a black hat with cockade, blue tunic edged with red with red cuffs, and red and gold braid epaulettes.

J.J. Watson. The Association viewed radical activity, centred round New College, with great suspicion. With the outbreak of war members sought to establish a local militia.

The Tower Hamlets militia were using London Fields for drill in 1753. There had been a volunteer militia established during the American War of Independence in 1777, with sixty-three men under Captain Toulmin (several generations of Toulmins were local doctors) and it may have helped deter local looting at the time of the anti-Catholic Gordon riots in 1780. The Association established two companies each of sixty men under Captains Williams and Samuel Dobree. The men were volunteers who paid for their own uniform, a blue coat with red facings and gold braid, black shoes and gaiters and black hats with black plumes and red and white cockades. Other costs were met by subscriptions. Activities consisted mostly of twice-weekly drill and target practice at the tile kilns at Upper Clapton, though the corps were called upon to suppress London riots in August 1794. Lack of funds led to the disbandment of Dobree's company in 1799 and with the temporary peace of Amiens in 1802, the remaining company was also stood down. When war resumed in 1803 the Association revived the volunteers, the bulk of whom were drawn from the lower orders – gardeners, servants, carpenters and shoemakers. Just how much use the volunteers and the county militia (paid for from local rates) would have been is questionable. In 1804 there was a sham fight at Wood Green, which nearly became a real one when the Hackney volunteers refused to join their colleagues from Stoke Newington in representing the French. There was little firing discipline and wadding from the Hackney men's guns struck their Islington companions, causing disorder and finally a brawl, which was broken up with difficulty. The struggle resulted in the only battle honours won by the volunteers – the accidental bayoneting of an Islington volunteer through the leg. Nelson's victory at Trafalgar removed the threat of invasion and funds for the volunteers had all but dried up by 1809. Disbandment is said to have followed two years later.

Hackney's population in 1801 of 12,730 rose to 16,771 in 1821 and 31,047 in 1831 and in uneven spurts between slumps, building development increased. The late eighteenth century saw isolated examples of speculative building. It was difficult to lease manorial land for terms of sufficient length to allow developers to recoup their investment and some estate owners gradually enfranchised their land, as the Cass trustees did between 1779 and 1786. Leases of manorial land and copyholds in Hackney could be made for up to thirty-one years, but this was too short a term to secure sound building from an investor. Enfranchisements increased in the nineteenth century as development proceeded. This chapter concludes by looking at examples of development in each area of Hackney before the major periods of Victorian growth.

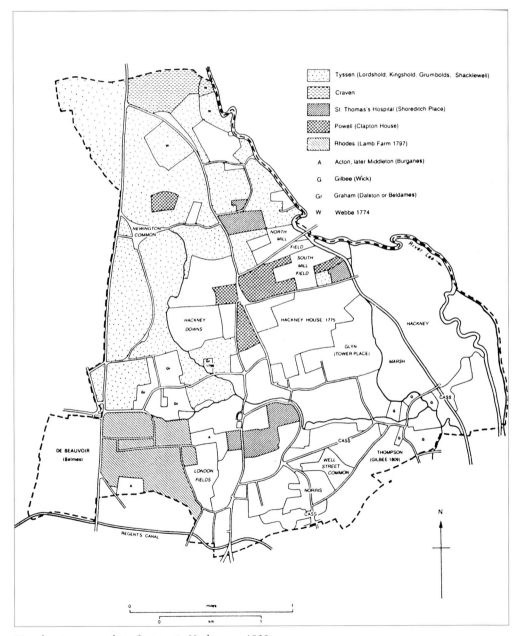

Map showing ownership of estates in Hackney, c. 1830.

Thomas Tryon.

In Hackney village and Mare Street, some back streets like Jerusalem Square and Baxter's Court dated from about 1700. The Mare Street area was the most populous in Hackney in 1720. Typical of early eighteenth-century housing was the pair later numbered nos 134–6, south of the Well Street junction, one of which was home to the traveller Celia Fiennes up to her death in 1741. Early nineteenth-century development started on the St Thomas Hospital estate in 1809 when Robert Collins built the Paragon. After his bankruptcy his former partner, attorney John Scott, began houses on the west side of Chatham Place in about 1815, extending to both sides of the road by 1820. To the north, carpenter John Musgrove replaced stabling with houses on Buck House Lane (later Cold Bath Lane and now the eastern end of Kenmure Road) in 1800; Musgrove also built third-rate houses at the south corner of the lane in 1812. To the south an early developer was the merchant Thomas Tryon, a self-made man who had started as a Gloucester shepherd boy and had come to London with his savings made from selling sheep to serve as a caster-maker's apprentice in Bridewell dock. By 1692 he was a merchant and Hackney landowner and on his death he left several houses on Tryon's Place (the western end of the present Tudor Road) and a little volume of memoirs combined with some injunctions 'proper for women to observe'. Haggerston brickmaker John Waxham was building on Lamb Lane shortly after 1713, and Jacob Alvares may have built some of the seven houses he owned in 1730.

After the governors of St Thomas Hospital decided to build on the site of the former Grove House, south of Morning Lane, they also leased land to Robert Collins, who was responsible for laying out St Thomas Square in 1771–2. Early residents included the minister Richard Price, who lived at no. 2 from 1786 to his death in 1791. To the north Joseph Spackman built 224–238 Mare Street shortly after 1780, which still stands to the north of the later Darnley Road. The bow-fronted house at the south end was home to Benjamin Clarke, local doctor and antiquarian from 1850 to 1863, and thereafter to a succession of doctors until the late 1970s. In the Well Street vicinity St Thomas Place was built by Thomas Pearson between 1805 and 1807 and

The southern end of Spackman's Terrace, with Benjamin Clarke's former house on the end, photographed looking north from Darnley Road in about 1905.

Denmark Place on the south side by Hylton Dennis Hacon in 1810. At the bottom end of Mare Street James Benson was responsible for Cambridge Row (later part of Cambridge Terrace in the 1790s). Close to the parish boundary on the east side were John and North Streets (later Vyner and Northiam streets respectively), consisting of very small houses close to the canal, with damp basement rooms. The area rapidly became some of the poorest housing in Hackney. Broadway Market's first housing, in Duncan Place, had been named by 1811.

Large-scale development began in Dalston at the west end of Dalston Lane and on the high road. Robert Sheldrick was active on Rhodes land on the south side of Dalston Lane in 1807 and built Dalston Terrace between 1813 and 1816. By 1831 the street was lined with houses east to the hamlet itself. On Kingsland Road terraces completed by 1821 included Kingsland Place, south of Dalston Lane, and Kingsland Crescent, under construction in 1793. William and Thomas Rhodes were leasing out houses in the newly completed Richmond Road in 1833, the first part of the development of their Lamb Farm estate. Much of the De Beauvoir estate had been leased by William Rhodes in 1821 and was planned as a grid pattern with four squares at each corner of the estate linked by intersecting roads at a central octagon. However, his proposed paving and lighting bill of 1823 was abandoned and piecemeal development ensued, mostly on the southern part of the estate and on the edges, like the west side of De Beauvoir Square and Lockner Street. When Richard Benyon inherited the estate in 1821 he decided to regain control of the estate and there was a lengthy legal battle which Benyon, who changed his name to Benyon de Beauvoir, eventually won in 1834. Subsequently De Beauvoir and his estate manager altered Rhodes's layout and they built houses that proved to be grander than the area could support. De Beauvoir Square was in social decline from the 1840s and it was not until the 1970s that it began to regain some of the social standing the original developer had intended.

At Shacklewell Charles Everard, who had acquired houses on the former manor site, was leasing further new houses on the site in 1762. He held most of the property on the north-west side of the Shacklewell Lane and at the north end a house that had been the poorhouse of St Bride's, Fleet Street. John Godfrey was building houses on the corner with Love Lane (later Norfolk and then Cecilia Road) in 1785, completed in 1799. The Revd John Hindle also built some houses on the south side after 1787, and another John Hindle and Thomas Greenwood were both active between 1811 and 1814. At the north-east end Milton House was briefly home to the composer Vincent Novello in 1823. North of Dalston Lane, the high road was built up with terraces and the Rhodes brothers were leasing new houses in Prospect Terrace near the site of West Hackney church in 1818.

Stamford Hill's height and comparative distance from the busier areas of the parish made it a desirable place to live. Cedar House, on the corner with Clapton Common, dated from 1760 and four adjoining houses, including Warwick House, had been completed by 1766. By contrast the west side of Stoke Newington High Street was densely developed by 1765. At the rear, and fronting on to Stoke Newington Common, Henry Sanford, a brewer, built twenty-nine houses forming Sanford Place and Terrace after 1775. A horseshoe-shaped pond next to the Birdcage public house was drained for building in 1793.

The destruction of Hackney House is likely to have been followed by some rebuilding of the Five Houses, a row of detached properties that lay between the estate and Lower Clapton Road. The middle house, owned by Thomas Boddington, which had been leased to Nathan Rothschild, was demolished, probably by William Amory, who acquired the property in 1822. He used the

Cedar House with members of the Aveling family on the front lawn, *c.* 1900.

site of the house as an approach to a new building of five bays called The Hall, built on former Hackney House estate land. To the east, also on the former estate land, lay the Priory, a castellated Gothic house with an approach from Brooksby's Walk. To the west Clapton Square dated from 1816 and building was still in progress. Residents in 1817 included the manorial steward Thomas Tebbutt and in 1821 the surveyor William Hurst Ashpitel, who lived in a villa in the north-east corner which was demolished in 1901. Additional building work in the vicinity of Clapton Pond included Brooke House Row on the west side, north of Kates Lane (the present Kenninghall Road), which was completed by 1760. To the north Beecholme House, opposite Brooke House, was the family home of Major John André, executed for spying by the Americans in the War of Independence in 1780. Beyond Kates Lane development, to add to three isolated rows on land held by the Webbe family since the seventeenth century, saw the construction of rows of cottages in the present Oldhill Street by 1774. On Kates Lane itself there were a number of small crowded short streets, which housed over seventy labourers' families by 1821, mostly employed on the brickfields. In 1827 there were complaints of drinking, Sunday shopping and gambling in the brickfields but the rest of Upper Clapton was regarded as genteel. However, it was not on the main turnpike route from Lea Bridge Road through Lower Clapton, which may have encouraged some residents to move north in the mid-eighteenth century. Long rows of houses included Buccleuch Terrace on the east side of the common, built in about 1825, and Summit Place, north of the Swan. In 1831 the only gap was soon to be taken for the construction of Champion Place. Mixed with the terraces were villas like Stainforth House and Cintra House, and east of the common were a group of houses on Spring Place, Springfield and Mount Pleasant Lane. Some, like Spring Hill House, which dated in part from the sixteenth century, may have incorporated parts of earlier buildings but were remodelled by later owners. To the north of the

The north-east corner of Clapton Square in 1892. Photograph, Alfred Braddock.

common Craven Lodge had been built for John Craven, probably between 1806 and 1818. In 1840, by which time the richest inhabitants had started to leave Hackney, it was one of the seats praised for the quality of its landscaped grounds.

One of the earliest Homerton developers was Edward Brooksby, who bought land in 1725 and left several houses completed in Brooksby's Walk on his death in 1753. Also active in the same area was brickmaker William Pratt who was building in the vicinity of Homerton High Street in the 1740s and 1750s. Later development included Sutton Place, built by William Collins in 1809, which added to the respectable property in Upper Homerton (later Urswick Road) and Homerton Row. Homerton had begun a slow social decline but this was not to accelerate until the 1850s with the expansion of the workhouse, Berger's paint factory and the construction of the railway to the south.

In South Hackney the Cass estate leased land in 1786 to William Gigney, a baker who built houses on the corner of Well Street and a new road that later became Cassland Road. Gigney went bankrupt in 1790 and the undertenants of his successor – William Fellowes, John Shillitoe and Thomas Pickering, James Jackson – built Hackney Terrace (20–54 Cossland Road) between 1796 and 1801, complete with its own stable block to the east and shared garden lawn at the rear.

In 1832 Hackney's inhabitants' meetings were much taken up with the trials and tribulations of the passing of the Reform Act. Some who were not wholehearted about reform supported the passage of the act, including Benjamin Clarke's father. When the act was finally passed the poor rejoiced, although there was little in it for them, and any opponents like Mr Wilson, who lived in the house on Mare Street that is now the Lansdowne Club, would have liked to put up their shutters in mourning, but to do so would have invited smashed windows. But although there was nothing in the Reform Act for the working classes, it did represent the beginning of a new era – for the country and for Hackney.

4. PARISH GOVERNMENT

From Tudor times Hackney was governed by parish meetings. The earliest recorded meeting dates from 1541 and the main recorded business was the election of parishioners to serve as churchwardens, sidesmen, surveyors of the highways and collectors for the poor. From 1581 only one churchwarden was elected – the other was chosen by the vicar. Wealthy parishioners could escape parish duties by making a monetary payment to the parish. The first record of the levy of parish rates dates from 1605.

Parish meetings were well attended and could be rowdy affairs; this did not suit the vicar or the better class of inhabitants, who petitioned the Bishop of London. The Bishop granted a faculty to create a select vestry in 1613, which consisted of the rector, vicar, assistant curate, the churchwardens and thirty-two named parishioners. Select vestries were common elsewhere but normally resulted in the ending of meetings for all parishioners. However in Hackney the open meetings continued and by the early eighteenth century, when the first surviving minutes begin, provided a forum for debate and action on a wide range of issues, from the state of local roads to the need for a parish workhouse. In December 1768 the meeting even found time to note the 'great inconvenience' caused by presence of a set of strolling players at the Mermaid alehouse in Church Street and threatened them with prosecution if they 'do not give over playing and quit this parish'.

Church business had been conducted in Church or Urswick's House but moved to a room in the church after Church House was taken for the Free School in 1616. The principal business of the vestry – and concerns of the parish meetings – were the maintenance of the church; regulation of parochial charities and associated parish property; the parish school; administration of the poor law; law and order (gradually taken over from the manor); roads; and funding these functions through raising church, highway and poor rates. Not all these functions were wholly the responsibility of the parish and some were taken over by *ad hoc* bodies or run by contractors from time to time. The elected officers and vestrymen were assisted by paid officials. The earliest was the parish clerk, in existence before 1625, when a dispute confirmed the vestry's right to elect the successful candidate. In 1711 the post was combined with that of vestry clerk. Sextons were appointed before 1632 and the post was sometimes occupied by women. A beadle was first appointed in 1657 'for the preventing of multiplying of the poor', though this was a forlorn hope and it was the beadles who multiplied – going to two in 1732 and three by 1810. From 1726 to 1836 the parish employed searchers to examine corpses. In 1730 parish employees consisted of the vestry clerk, a beadle, an organist, a sextoness, a clock minder, an organ bellows blower, a churchyard keeper and a midwife.

The parish was not always fortunate in its servants. In September 1799 the inhabitants' meeting considered the position of their parish clerk, William Trulock, intending to dismiss him for 'notorious drunkeness'. Trulock was summoned in person but sent his wife instead, claiming that he had two 'apoplectick fits'; the parishioners, however, were not to be deterred. The vestry clerk, accompanied by the curate Mr Parroissein and his clerk, were sent round to Trulock's house forthwith and found him not so ill as he had claimed. A series of charges were put to him. Asked if he could deny the charge of being a notorious drunkard, Trulock replied 'No – I have been drunken, but notorious goes a long way'. But he was unable to deny a range of other charges, including being drunk at the funeral of the former vicar, Mr Cornthwaite, and forgetting notices of other funerals – 'I do not recollect anything about it'. A plea that he would make amends seemed somewhat lame and he was dismissed forthwith.

Tudor legislation had made poor relief a parish responsibility, which was doubtless regarded as onerous and expensive by Hackney's vestry. The destitute, aged or unemployed and unmarried mothers were all to be given financial aid – relief – by their proven parish of settlement. This was not necessarily their place of birth; it could also be where the applicant had lived for forty days with the knowledge of the vestry, had served an apprenticeship, or had been in service or employment for over a year. Anyone applying for relief would be examined by the local justice of the peace and if he or she did not meet any of these conditions, then the justice would make an order of removal to the last place of settlement. Like any other parish, Hackney vestry was concerned to ensure that expenses of the poor did not bear too heavily on the rates. Single pregnant women were often subjected to removal, for if a child was born within the parish it automatically gained a settlement and became a parochial responsibility. In the sixteenth century some funds were raised by collectors for specific purposes, for example in 1581 for a fatherless child, but there were also payments of pensions to look after the young or the sick, intended to number no more than fifteen in 1628. The poor also received gifts, usually bread or coal, paid for from the rents of land left to the parish or purchased with charitable bequests. One such donation by Valentine Poole in 1624, of the five-acre Butfield, south of Well Street, was known by association as Hackney poor's land in the nineteenth century.

The cost of poverty gradually rose through the eighteenth century. Faced with a demand to contribute to relief in Stepney in 1676, the vestry claimed that the burden of its own poor was already too great. In 1708 bread was distributed to seventy-four people and in 1710 it was ordered that all the poor should wear badges, with the exception of Henry Rowe (impoverished descendant of the once mighty lords of the manor), as a sign of a new determination to deter applications for charity. Rising rates were required to meet the cost of money payments. As early as 1598 a payment had been made to 'the poor house' and one child was sent to a workhouse outside Hackney in 1709. The idea of workhouses dated back to the sixteenth century and they were originally intended to ensure that those paupers perceived as idle but able could be set to work. Finished goods could then be sold and assist in the cost of poor relief. In the seventeenth century each local workhouse required an act of parliament to be established but legislation of 1722 allowed a parish or group of parishes to rent or buy premises for the purpose, run either by a parish employee or a contractor. Relief could then be denied to anyone who refused to become an inmate and the parish had the option of residential care for the sick, aged, infirm and orphaned children.

The 1722 act may have concentrated thinking in Hackney. Deliberations in 1728–9 concluded on the construction of a workhouse near Bowling Green House (later on Chatham Place) but this came to nothing and eventually a house on Homerton High Street was leased from John Evans in 1732 and repaired. It was too small by the late 1730s and in 1741 the parish leased a gabled house on the south side of Homerton High Street (whose site forms part of the recently demolished

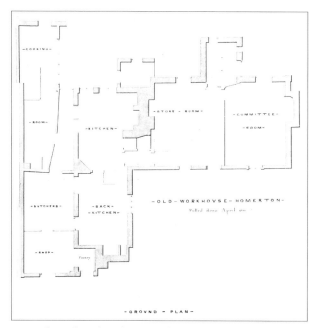

Floor plan of Hackney parish workhouse, drawn by
B. Saunders, 1841.

Hackney hospital), which was rented from George Milborne. Recorded as being owned by the Denham family in 1624, it probably dated from the late sixteenth century. The vestry added sheds on the site to house additional paupers and turned their purchase into a loan in 1768.

Initially the house was managed by the parish and held between forty-one to seventy-four people, but seeking to cut costs it was contracted out in 1753 to Richard Charles, who agreed to act as workhouse master for the sum of 2s 4d per pauper. Charles agreed to clothe the inmates, though the parish met the costs of a midwife and clothing children going out to apprenticeship. Charles could keep any money he made from sale of goods, which was better than his previous arrangement. In return Charles undertook to provide 'wholesome meat and drink', a clean shirt for the men and a clean shift for the women once a week. The vestry's workhouse management committee had also drawn up printed rules, probably just prior to Charles' contract, and these are available in facsimile from Hackney Archives Department.

Charles proved to be successful workhouse master, though it is regrettable that he destroyed all the records of how the workhouse had been run before his contract began. He was gradually able to raise his rates. In 1754 he complained 'that he was out of pocket by reason of the dearness of provisions and burying the dead' and was able to charge an additional 4d per head for clothes, though to keep the workhouse committee sweet he provided a fire in their meeting room. The parish also met repairs and additions to the workhouse – the paupers were treated to the luxury of a new cold bath in October 1754. Charles was back again in December 1755, claiming that 'the great age and infirmity of the people in the workhouse make them incapable of assisting him or themselves' and got another 2d per head, and made the committee pay for their own fire! Charles died in 1759 and his wife Betty took over on a temporary basis. Betty Charles married

Hackney parish workhouse from Homerton High Street, 1841.

Hackney parish workhouse yard, 1841.

Richard Maddicks in 1761 and the newlyweds took on the contract in full. Clearly the parish members were still satisfied, for in 1760 they had indignantly rebutted charges 'that all the children who have been born or admitted very young to the workhouse had died', but their own figures show that of seven children admitted aged under three months, two died; of seven aged three months to two years, four died; while of the twenty-five children born in the house, four had died; perhaps the parish could argue that the mortality rates among admissions were no higher than would have been expected among the children of the poor.

The numbers of poor continued to rise and the parish obtained an act of parliament in 1763 to set up a board of trustees, who appointed Matthew Arnold as workhouse master in 1764 at the rate of 3s per pauper. But less than a year later Arnold was mostly absent from the house and had left it in the incapable hands of a Mrs Smith. Arnold was dismissed when he refused to sack Smith and the trustees took direct control of the house, appointing a salaried master on £30 per annum. The workhouse was enlarged in 1775 to cater for 220 people but this was insufficient by 1807, when conditions were so bad that the vicar of Hackney urged a move to a new site. A new shed was added to extend the working area in 1811 and further additions were made in 1813 to cope with 280 inmates. Some of the older buildings were falling into disrepair and the children's workshop was replaced by a new three-storey building, with bedrooms, sick ward, drying rooms and a workshop. The rules were held to be insufficiently harsh but the only improvement a committee could suggest was imposing a special dress on unmarried mothers.

In 1822 rumours of worsening conditions prompted a special investigation, which found that many of the rules were being broken. There was free association between men and women with the result that illegitimate births in the house had risen. The walls were so low that inmates could come and go at will, resulting, it was claimed, in a spate of local burglaries. Beds in the wards were vermin-ridden and there was no adequate water supply for the women. The schoolmistress was often too drunk to teach at all. By 1831 Hackney claimed to have remedied these defects and to run a 'model workhouse' holding 102 men, 153 women, 80 boys and

Spurstowe's almshouses, seen from the Grove (site of the present Hackney Town Hall). Watercolour by George Hawkins, *c.* 1830.

60 girls. Out relief was provided to a further 398 pensioners and 35 children being nursed but the buildings still had no proper school accommodation or place for worship and real remedies had to wait the formation of the Hackney Poor Law Union in 1837.

Some instances of poverty were also helped by Hackney's many charitable bequests, the result of donations from wealthy inhabitants from the early seventeenth century onwards. In the early eighteenth century there was an annual distribution of royal bounty money and by 1830 there were a further thirty-one bequests. Some provided for the distribution of bread or coals, like Thomas Heron's gift of 1603, while others combined donations to the poor with funds for the upkeep of bridges and fences (Margaret Audley's bequest of 1617), for the apprenticeship of local children (Henry Bannister's gift of 1625) or as monetary distributions to widows or those selected by the vestry. Funds came from rent charges on local estates or from donated land, which the parish owned and managed. In 1789–90 the total income from land and investments was £180, rising to £213 in 1800, but in that year only £101 was spent.

The most visible charitable bequests were the almshouse charities. The oldest was founded by Dr William Spurstowe, Hackney's former vicar, who continued to live in the parish after his ejection in 1662. He built six almshouses for widows in 1666 on part of his estate on the west side of the later Sylvester Path. His brother created a trust to run the almshouses and added land to the original gift, making a total of fourteen acres, which provided income. Vacancies were filled by the nomination of two almswomen from the parish, to be selected by Spurstowe's heirs until 1802, after which the parish acted alone. The almshouses were rebuilt in 1819, funded by

The original Monger's almshouse building, drawn by Robert Schnebbelie, 11 July 1815.

sale of stock and surplus charitable income. Inmates also received annual gifts of money from a further three local charities. Rent income was raised when the charity's estate was built on in the mid-1850s. The almshouse range lasted until 1966, when they were demolished and the site sold. A successor building with sixteen flats was completed at nos 36–8 Navarino Road and is still maintained by the parochial charity today.

In his will proved in 1669 Henry Monger left £400 and land in Well Street, together with a rent charge on land in Hackney Marsh, for the construction of six brick almshouses for men aged sixty or above. This gift was added to by Joanna Martin whose will of about 1679 gave two houses just to the west of the almshouses and rents to supplement pensions for the almspeople and to aid repairs. Sir John Cass acquired the charged marshland and Cass's widow, Dame Elizabeth, was nominating women for the almshouses in 1732, though she was asked to substitute men as women were not eligible under the terms of Monger's will. Dame Elizabeth's influence did ensure, however, that almsmen were able to bring their wives with them. The Cass Charity continued to run the almshouses until their right to do so was investigated by the vicar of Hackney, Archdeacon Watson, who successfully reasserted the parish's control. Unfortunately the parish reverted to the strict terms of the will, which ejected widows after the death of their husbands. The almshouses stood on the same site as their replacement, on the north side of Grove Street (now Church Crescent). They were in a poor condition by 1846 when the energetic Cass estate surveyor George Wales proposed the construction of a new road through the site, offering to build four new houses to provide rental and new almshouses on a triangle of land bounded by Grove Street, Cassland Road and the proposed road (the present Terrace Road). In the event the parish decided the site was too constricted and underestimated the cost of rebuilding the old almshouses. A problem with the boundary between the Cass estate and the almshouse land made the problem

Norris almshouses, from Victoria Park Road, shortly before demolition in 1967.

more complicated and in the event Wales proposed the arrangement that was finally accepted. The parish surrendered some land at the west end of the estate's endowed houses for the construction of Terrace Road and Wales secured the funding to rebuild all but two of the endowed houses (Blenheim Cottages, later nos 1–7 Church Crescent) in 1847–8. Wales also arranged the rebuilding of the almshouses themselves on the same site in 1848, meeting the difference between the £1,100 rebuilding cost and the £750 the charity could afford. Further modernization and alterations took place in 1969 and the almshouses are still in use today.

The problem of widows losing their places was partially addressed after the death of the first rector of South Hackney, Henry Handley Norris. In 1857 a combination of subscriptions, including a donation from his widow, funded the construction of four almshouses on land given by Norris's son on the west side of the junction of Victoria Park and Handley Roads. The inmates were to be single women aged sixty or above, members of the Church of England, with preference given to the widows of Monger's almsmen. The original gabled Tudor-style red-brick almshouses were demolished in 1968 and replaced by the present Norris Court, which provides sheltered accommodation for six couples and five single women.

Thomas Wood, Bishop of Lichfield, bought land in Clapton in about 1653 and built an almshouse range for ten widows aged sixty or above. In his will of 1692 he left a rent charge for pensions and to pay for a chaplain to read prayers twice a week. Wood's heirs continued to

Bishop Wood's almshouses and children. Photograph, Alfred Braddock, *c.* 1900.

appoint almswomen until 1798. The almshouses, originally consisting of a central range of six one-roomed tenements and projecting wings of two tenements in each, were restored in 1930. The chapel at the north end, repaired in 1855 by the vicar of the nearby St James church, J.C. Powell, had seats for ten people and was claimed to be Britain's smallest chapel when the almshouses were reopened after wartime requisitioning in 1948.

Hackney's third set of almshouses for eight poor families with small children were built by Thomas Cooke, a Stoke Newington resident, on wasteland at the edge of Stoke Newington Common, which he had leased in 1740. Cooke's will, leaving land to support the charity, was found to be invalid but his family continued to maintain it on a voluntary basis and the almshouses were known as Cooke's Rents. Cooke's original lease from the lord of the manor was due to expire in 1839 but two years beforehand the almshouses were conveyed to West Hackney's vestry, who passed on the management to a committee of subscribers. The almshouses were rebuilt in 1841 and renamed the West Hackney almshouses. These buildings were demolished in 1885 when their site became a school playground and new buildings were put up on what became Northwold Road. Now called West Hackney House, these provide eight tenements on two floors round a central hall. The inmates also receive money from a fund created in the memory of Charles Fisher Yates, a former mayor of Hackney, who died in 1945.

The parish also had some responsibilities for local roads. Hackney had two historic main roads running through it. The Roman Ermine Street ran through Shoreditch and formed the border between Hackney and Stoke Newington. It was met at Shoreditch church by Old Street. In medieval times there was some recognition that the maintainance of roads carrying national traffic required financial help and there were triennial grants of pavage made by the Crown for road repair on the Hackney to Tottenham stretch between 1365 and 1373. Local roads and bridges, however, were the responsibility of local people. A jury in 1512 found that Temple Mills Bridge was in a bad state of repair and that William Beye or Tey of Colchester, who owned the piece of Hackney land that had been charged with its upkeep, ought to take appropriate action.

This left the majority of roads without a framework for maintenance so an act of 1555 laid down that each parish should be responsible for roads within its boundaries. All parishioners were required to provide four days of labour on local roads, under the supervision of surveyors of the highways. In 1563 the number of days was increased to six and in 1587, after further amendments, the principle was established as permanent.

Under the acts the surveyor, who usually served for a year as an unpaid officer, had to ensure that the statute labour was done – or that paid substitutes provided – and that the roads were kept free of obstructions. Parishes that failed to carry out their duties could be presented at county quarter sessions and fined. During the Commonwealth period statute labour was abolished and replaced by levied rates and though this lapsed after 1660, the principle of substituting a highway rate to supplement statute labour was introduced, though it did not become a permanent power until 1693. Bridges, especially those that crossed rivers or streams on parish boundaries, were usually a county responsibility, or at least liable in principle to county support. In 1839 Hackney's Highways Board, having discovered through the good offices of antiquarian and board member George Offor the decrepit state of Temple Mills Bridge in 1512, wrote to the Essex Justices of the Peace in an attempt to get them to fund repairs but received a dusty answer. There was also some manorial involvement and overflowing ditches and middens blocking lanes could be referred to the homage jury, but the frequency with which the same complaint recurred at successive courts in the seventeenth century suggested that by that stage the manorial court had little practical power.

Parochial maintenance had many pitfalls. Because of the expense and trouble, surveyors were anxious to serve for a year only so there was no continuity or accumulation of expertise. Local people would evade the period of statute labour if possible and local benefactions could at best be only a partial solution. For example David Doulben, former Vicar of Hackney and Bishop of Bangor, left £30 in his will of 1633 to repair the footpath from Clapton to Shoreditch (part of which forms the present Market Porter's route). But local measures could not keep pace with the increase in wagon traffic on the major roads from the late seventeenth century onwards. Dust in summer and deep mud in winter, together with flooding, led to accidents and loss of goods, as well as delays to travellers by horse and carriage.

In 1713 the state of Ermine Street between Shoreditch and Enfield led to a petition to parliament by inhabitants of the seven parishes that the road passed through, claiming it was 'so worn out by frequent travelling therein, that it is very dangerous in the winter season'. A second petition from farmers, waggoners, pack carriers, stagecoachmen, carters, higglers and others who travelled the route claimed that 'the petitioners are often damaged by their goods being overturned in the said road, occasioned by the badness thereof'.

The solution was to seek the sanction of an act of parliament to create a trust to maintain roads that were beyond the means of a single parish. The first such act of 1663 had come about through the petition of the parishioners of Standon in Hertfordshire for a section of the Great North Road, which allowed justices of the peace to erect gates, collect tolls, appoint officials and supervise repairs. In 1706 the first trust was established, where trustees took on the role previously performed by the justices. This became the standard model and it was this pattern that was adopted for the establishment of the Stamford Hill Turnpike Trust in 1713.

The Stamford Hill toll gate and lodge, *c.* 1865.

Under the provisions of the act, forty-six trustees were empowered to appoint surveyors and collectors, dig drains and extract gravel from private land and collect tolls. The Trust was envisaged as a temporary measure but the £3,500 spent in the first year exceeded the income from tolls and the initial thirteen-year term would be inadequate to repay the resultant loan. A further act was required a year later and the turnpike trust had its term extended still further by later legislation. Statute labour was still required, though two parishes on its route, Hackney and Shoreditch, agreed to levy highway rates to commute their shares. The additional legislation also required toll gates to be put on side roads and to prevent farmers whose land adjoined the turnpike allowing travellers to pass over it and evade the toll gates. A curious clause in an act of 1728 allowed the Trustees to flood low parts of the road in winter, based on a theory that mud could be washed off the roads, leaving only the gravel. There seems to have been little need to artificially flood the roads, for in 1763 a Select Committee on Metropolitan Turnpikes heard that 'the waters are frequently out in the said road so as to prevent passengers from travelling and have continued so for some hours; that the mail has been stopped several times . . . [and] that no money has ever been laid out or method taken by the Trust to carry off the said waters'. Even after fifty years of the Trust, much remained to be done.

The Stamford Hill Trust was extended to take in Green Lanes in 1789. By then there were two other turnpike trusts covering roads in Hackney. The Hackney Turnpike Trust was established in 1738 for Hackney Road, Cambridge Heath Road and northwards covering Mare Street and Lower and Upper Clapton Roads. The Hackney Trust took over Dalston Lane after 1799. To the east the Lea Bridge and Road Trust, established in 1757, built a new bridge to replace Jeremy's Ferry and a new road to Leyton to the north of the old one to the ferry.

The Trusts funded their capital works, which included bridge construction and road widening, from loans. Income came from the toll gates and by the end of the eighteenth century there were six of these. The Stamford Hill Trustees had gates at the top of Kingsland Road and

The second Lea Bridge, from an engraving produced shortly after the bridge was completed in 1820.

at Stamford Hill where there was also a weighing machine, which worked like a giant pair of scales enabling additional charges to be levied for overweight carts. The Hackney Trustees had gates at the Clapton junction with Lea Bridge Road (from 1758), at Shoreditch (at the beginning of Hackney Road), Cambridge Heath (at the other end of Hackney Road), and Dalston Lane (from 1770). There was one gate and toll house only on Lea Bridge Road, on the Hackney side of the River Lea, just before the bridge. The charges and the wait at each gate were a problem with turnpikes right from the start. Evasion of income by using neighbouring fields was a problem and so too were the new roads that were beginning to be constructed from the early nineteenth century onwards.

If the burden of road maintenance had been shifted from the parochial purse, there still remained the question of road safety. Turnpikes were unlit and subject to lurking highwaymen and there are several reports of robberies on Kingsland Road, like the one in 1728 of a Hackney stagecoach near Shoreditch church, which later resulted in the capture of the robber, an upholsterer. There was a need for lights and for watchmen. The Hackney Turnpike Trustees acquired the power to provide both in 1755 and put five oil lamps up in Church Street in the following year. The Stamford Hill Trustees followed suit in 1774 but the acquisition of this power did not necessarily mean its execution. In March 1767 Hackney's Lighting and Watching Trustees appointed a committee of their members to represent to the Turnpike Trustees 'the hardship to the inhabitants of this parish to light the turnpike through the Town of Hackney at the expense of the parish' and to seek financial support. Watch huts were provided along the routes of turnpikes and watchmen carried guns (Daniel Lee was sacked by the Hackney Trustees for losing his gun in 1780).

The parish also maintained responsibility for the remaining roads and footpaths and these continued to be under the supervision of the elected surveyor of the highways. The surveyor was under the general direction of the vestry and parish meetings and regularly reported to the inhabitants' meetings and members concerned with road and footpath management. This

Lea Bridge toll gate and lodge, *c.* 1865.

could range from a yard in Clapton claimed by its owner as private, and blocked with a gate and two large dogs in 1765, to the use of Back Road (now Clarence Road) as a kind of early rat run in 1771. This prompted the meeting to declare that Back Lane was not a public way from Clapton to Church Street but a private one for occupants of the Downs and Shacklewell. It was not wide enough for two coaches to pass and the parish had no intention of having to spend money to maintain it, so posts were placed at the Downs end, settling the problem for the next seventy years.

The meeting even established a committee to inspect footpaths in 1771 and it reported on the major problems four years later. Obstacles included new houses and the efforts of the calico printers and 'whitsters' (cloth bleachers) by High Bridge. Here, a footbridge by Coney Hole had gone and a dog kennel, complete with a very large chained dog, had been substituted by the calico printers. Trenches had been cut across the path by the whitsters and a Mr Web had built a dock for his tile kiln and omitted to provide any means of crossing it. Bridges, including the vexed Temple Mills Bridge, were a regular concern. In 1802 the Vestry Clerk stated he believed (like the later Highways Board) that the bridge was a county responsibility, and a later search nineteen years later could claim to find no record of the parish having repaired it for the last hundred years. Diversion or disruption to footpaths became even more of an issue in fields being worked for brick-earth. There was more than one disagreement between William Rhodes and the parish. In 1812 the surveyors demolished a wall across a footpath from Dalston to Kingsland across Lamb Farm. Rhodes threatened a legal case but the parish stood firm, informing him that if he blocked one path, then he should provide another. Similar problems were experienced with a Mr Hobson whose brick-earth excavations disrupted the course of Love Lane (which occupied roughly the course of the southern half of Cecilia Road and the

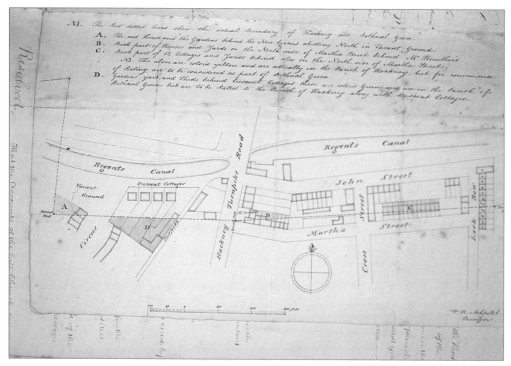

The newly developed roads lying just south of Regent's Canal from a plan in Hackney's inhabitants' meeting minutes of April 1826, drawn up to determine whether Hackney could claim them for rating purposes.

western part of Downs Park Road to Shacklewell) in 1824. Hobson had still not repaired the lane – to the disruption of the romantic? – a year later.

The trouble with brick-earth diggers was symptomatic of a change in emphasis from footpaths to new roads. In principle the parish would not accept responsibility to maintain newly built roads unless all work had been completed. In 1825 they agreed to adopt John Street, south of Regents Canal, but refused to take on North Street (later Northiam Street) until 'all the buildings are complete and the heavy traffic of drawing materials for brickmaking through the same is put a stop to'. The following year the area was the subject of an agreement with Bethnal Green parish, since developments in Martha Street on one side of Cambridge Heath Road and Crescent Cottages on the other straddled the parish border, and the householders would not have relished paying two sets of rates.

Changes to road administration and law and order took place in the 1820s. Individual turnpike trusts in the Hackney area had considerably improved the roads, though pipe-laying by the Imperial Gas Company and the East London Water Works Company prior to 1824 had caused disruption. However, the multiplicity of gates and standards of charges combined further increases in traffic. After a parliamentary enquiry, thirteen turnpike trusts, including the Stamford Hill and Hackney trusts, were combined to form the Metropolis Road Commission in 1827. In 1829 Hackney parish was opposed to the Metropolitan Police Act of that year, since it felt that its own local watch force had tackled the problem of local crime. Six months later it was claimed that the Metropolitan Police had proved 'wholly unsatisfactory to the inhabitants of the parish' as there had been more offences against property in six months than in the preceding two years, and the 150 men comprising the winter night watch, who had helped keep the streets safe, were now likely to become a charge on the parish poor rates. Just how efficient Hackney's watch really was may be open to question: in April 1828 two watchmen were sacked for standing by while a horse and cart had passed them one Sunday morning, laden with lead stolen from a local house. The theft was only discovered when another patrol found the robbers openly cutting up the lead in Ashpital's brickfield, later in the afternoon.

Hackney's own management of roads was to change in the following decade. The select vestry and the parish meetings had merged in 1833 and two years later Hackney adopted the Highways Act of 1835 and created a Highways Board, to which the surveyor now reported. This had eighteen members and first met in April 1836. It appointed a clerk, a solicitor, rate collectors and an assistant surveyor. In 1837 the Board created four district committees, for Clapton, Hackney, South Hackney and West Hackney, to provide closer supervision of each area. It took up the old issues of footpaths, Temple Mills Bridge and even the issue of Back Lane. In 1839 the eager assistant surveyor had removed the posts put up in 1771 and the carriages had promptly resumed using it in preference to Lower Clapton Road, producing noise and dust that 'make the back parts of the houses scarcely habitable', claimed the outraged inhabitants of the west side of that part of Lower Clapton Road. They added that 'the exposure of the gardens to the men riding in the different vehicles make it scarcely fit for the female part of families to walk in them.' Faced with the pressure of the well-to-do, the Board reinstated the posts, but by that time it was too late and in June 1840 they were summonsed to Worship Magistrate Court, where they lost their case and were ordered to remove the posts for good.

From the 1840s onwards, adoption of new streets increased and there are regular appearances in the records by men like John Lake, managing the development of De Beauvoir Town, and George Wales, surveyor to the Sir John Cass Charity. In 1848 Wales had occasion to complain of an excess bill from the Assistant Surveyor, Mr Woodward, and on investigation the Board found that Woodward had been taking fees for private work. Wales had complained when he had been billed for work over and above these payments. Woodward was reprimanded by the Board and narrowly escaped dismissal. The Board was still concerned with the routine matters of obstruction and offence: in August 1848 these included mounds of earth dumped by the Tyssen estate in Cold Bath Lane (Kenmure Road); George Wales leaving a grating off in Water Lane (Morning Lane) for three weeks, causing flooding; and the problem of Mr Booth, a butcher of Kingsland, who was boiling the 'awfull of meat in Mr Hunt's yard, which is quite an annoyance to the neighbourhood'. There were signs that members recognized that their responsibilities could extend beyond the roads to the adjoining properties. In October 1839 Board members went to inspect Jerusalem Gardens, taking with them a medical officer working for the Hackney Union. This seems to have been justified, for while the road had been made up to a reasonable standard, the houses on the north side were low and damp and their cesspools were likely to be a health hazard if left unremedied. The owner, Mr Bradshaw, was to be threatened with a fine if improvements were not undertaken.

Responsibility for lighting the parish had been undertaken by Lighting and Watching Trustees, who were established in 1764, but only the minutes from 1828 to 1837 survive for the nineteenth century, though the Trustees continued to exist up to 1856. However, the age of the parish trust was coming to an end: from 1856 Hackney was included in the area of the Metropolitan Board of Works. The work of both the lighting and the highway trustees was taken over by a new District Board of Works, covering both Hackney and Stoke Newington, and concerned with the regulation of what was built alongside the roads, as well as the maintenance and lighting of the roads themselves. The new and extensive street developments had made the old principles of turnpike gates unworkable and with traveller and business complaints of delays at the gates rising, Clapton Gate was removed in 1856 and then all the commissioner's roads in Hackney and Stoke Newington were transferred to the District Board in 1863. All the gates went, with the exception of the one on Lea Bridge, as that trust survived until 1872, after which only some private roads remained gated, the last being a tollgate at Temple Mills, which survived until 1911.

The law required parishes to have their own fire engines in 1708 and Francis Tyssen offered to provide an engine funded by landowners which was proportionate to their rateable value. Hackney's first fire station was on the south side of the churchyard. The old engine was regularly repaired and part-exchanged for a new one in 1754. This was joined by a second larger machine in 1774. In 1823 this was replaced in turn and the old engine assigned to Kingsland. Hackney remained responsible for fire engines until 1865, when it handed over five engines tended by eight men to the newly formed Metropolitan Fire Brigade.

Firemen with the horse-drawn engine outside the Hackney fire station in Bodney Road. Photograph, George James, c. 1870.

5. A GOOD EDUCATION?

The first reference to a parochial schoolmaster in Hackney is in 1580 and William Snape left 40 shillings in his will proved in 1587 for the better maintenance of the grammar school. In 1613 the vestry appointed James Chrycton on the recommendation of the Chancellor of the Bishop of London. Chrycton was 'thoughtflye to teach the inhabitants' children of this parish of Hackney' grammar, writing and accounts, charging no more than 4*d* per week and no more than 2*d* for those learning grammar only. Teaching could be extended to those living outside Hackney and in their case there was no restriction on what fees could be charged. The parish school had the use of the Church House, the building in front of the church built by Christopher Urswick.

The parish school was augmented by a bequest under the terms of Margaret Audley's will of 1616, which left money to the Skinner's Company. Out of this they were to pay an annuity to the Hackney churchwardens, part of which was to pay for a schoolmaster. The bequest may have been intended to create a second school but in practice the twelve boy pupils were taught in Church House by the existing schoolmaster. The parish had varying success with the quality of their appointed masters. In March 1640 Mordekay Keydon was given his marching orders because of his 'neglect in keeping the school and teaching the children of the parish'. A later successor, Robert Skingle, was appointed in 1644 and given some pupil aid; one was to be designated to act as porter and cleaner. Skingle was in trouble in 1665 for failing to qualify any of the scholars for university. The churchwardens ordered him to resign but he refused and kept possession of the school. The parish resolved the matter and made Skingle the parish lecturer, giving the Sunday afternoon sermon. The two posts of lecturer and schoolmaster were supposed to be distinct but were not finally separated until the appointment of the antiquarian John Strype as lecturer in 1689.

Hackney was also building up a substantial reputation for its private schools. With a healthy reputation, situated in the country yet conveniently close to the city, and popular as a place of summer residence for visitors, Hackney also had a number of large houses built in the sixteenth century which were ideal for use as schools. John Salladine, a French schoolmaster, was a resident in 1627 and a rich city orphan was abducted from a Mrs Winch's boarding house ten years later. As a small child Samuel Pepys boarded at Hackney and on a return visit in April 1667 went to Hackney church, 'chiefly to see . . . the young ladies of the schools, whereof there is a great store, very pretty . . .'. Among those running girls' boarding schools was the Presbyterian Mrs Elizabeth Salmon in 1648, probably from the house in Clapton later used by Benjamin Morland and the Newcomes. Mrs Salmon taught French, housewifery and polite accomplishments and her husband was able to claim a gallery in the church for the use of her pupils, who included the 'matchless Orinda', the poet Katherine Philips in 1639. Mary Perwich established her fashionable boarding school in Church Street in 1643 in a house that was

Susanna Perwich.

assessed as the second largest in the parish in 1664 and may have been the later Templars House. Mary and her husband Robert taught household skills and employed well-known masters to teach music and dancing. The skills of their daughter Susanna on the violin attracted distinguished audiences from London in the 1650s, though it may have been the Perwich's school that serving man Joseph Lister criticized in 1640 as merely for 'young gentlewomen to learn to play and dance and sing' and castigated the lack of daily prayers.

Among other girls' boarding school mistresses was Hannah Wooley, an early advocate of women's education, who moved there from Essex in 1655, and wrote two works on cookery, published in 1661 and 1664. In 1694 three of the thirteen well-known ladies' boarding schools in the country were at Hackney. Providing pews in Hackney's church became an increasing problem. Robert Perwich had been allowed to build his own gallery in the church in 1649 but in 1686 the parish forbade schools that had their own gallery from making use of pews in the body of the church. In the Restoration years girls' schools were criticized for frivolity and John Aubrey commented sourly that convent education had been preferable as Hackney schools taught girls pride and wantonness. The schools also made a satirical target for court dramatists, targeting the London citizens' daughters who made up much of the intake. In Thomas Shadwell's *The Humourists* of 1671 the Hackney-educated haberdasher's wife was portrayed as snobbish and in Wycherley's *The Gentleman Dancing Master* of 1672, the father keeps a close eye on his daughter, also from a Hackney school.

In 1715 Mrs Wallis, Mrs Hammond and Elizabeth Hutton all kept girls' boarding schools at Hackney. Mrs Hutton may have had the Black and White House, which was kept by Mary Roberts in 1747 and was to remain a school until it was demolished in 1795. It was probably the back door of the Black and White House that the young diarist Dudley Ryder came through in August 1715 and found the girls 'at first very merry with dancing but presently comes the schoolmistress and reproved them very severely for their having held discourse with a man and entertaining them upon a wall. One of the Lancashire girls talked very smartly to her again.' Later in the century Mrs Ranking hired a Frenchman for her boarders in Tryon's Place and in 1791 Mrs Larkham was advertising for her establishment at the pleasant and healthy village of Dalston:

> Young ladies are genteely and well boarded and taught all kinds of useful and fashionable needlework, the English and French languages gramatically, geography with the use of globes, history and several other branches of necessary and polite learning.

Mrs Larkham's price was 16 guineas a year and she also employed masters to teach writing, dancing, music and drawing. If the price seemed low, 'Mrs Larkham thinks it may not be improper to observe that great care will taken of the young ladies in point of board, education, health and morals as at any school in the kingdom', while cards of reference from parents of existing pupils would deal with the 'minutest enquiries of the most anxious or indulgent parent'.

Boys' schools also flourished in eighteenth-century Hackney. Early eighteenth-century schools could be dangerous places judging by a newspaper report of 1722.

Rear of the Black and White House, with the tower of St John at Hackney old church, as it would have appeared about 1750. From a watercolour attributed to T. Fisher, *c.* 1790.

A few days ago two Lads had some Words at Mr W's Boarding School in Hackney: the one being stronger than the other ty'd him up by his hands to a beam in his room, and after having stripped and beat him, he drew his sword and stabbed him in several places under the arm; which not content with the cruel youth exercised his penknife on him too. He then took him down and finding he was not despatched, hung him up again by the neck and so left him, but some other lad coming into the room just afterwards took him down; and he is now in a fair way of recovery. Let this caution all parents how they arm their children with swords, before they have discretion enough to rule their passions.

Not that there was any question of the boys having swords in the first place, for it was the upper classes that these schools sought to attract, especially Hackney's most famous private boys' school, Newcome's or Hackney School. Established by Benjamin Morland in an old house on Lower Clapton Road in about eight acres of grounds, it passed to his son-in-law Henry Newcome, probably in 1721 when Morland became high master of St Paul's School. Newcome, son of Hackney's vicar Peter Newcome, may have been a poor preacher but his school attracted the leading Whig patrons of the mid-eighteenth century, including the Cavendishes, the Fitzroys, the third and fourth Dukes of Devonshire and the second Earl of Hardwicke. The school was noted for its plays, produced annually from 1730, with prologues or epilogues given by famous actors of the day, including David Garrick in 1763. The school passed to Newcome's son Peter and ultimately to Peter's grandson, Richard, whom one pupil described as 'a bad schoolmaster, gouty and violent',who ran it until 1802. Later pupils included Stratford Canning, a pupil from 1792 to 1794, who recalled tree climbing, visits to a nearby pastry cooks' shop and excursions to the River Lea in the summer to bathe. Robert Creevy the diarist remembered the bullying and younger boys being sent out on cold November evenings 'to pilfer turnips from a neighbouring field, and many were the logs of firewood or kettles of boiling water I had to carry up the dark and winding staircase'. From the end of 1802 the school was run by C.T. Heathcote until it closed sometime between 1815 and 1819 and the site was

Newcomes or Hackney School from the rear. Engraving by Reeve, *c.* 1820.

eventually sold to the London Orphan Asylum. French featured highly in some curriculums. Isaac Coustell, a teacher in Hackney, brought out a French grammar in 1748. John Naudin claimed that only French was spoken in his Well Street establishment in 1775. Two possible successors Paul de la Pierre and a Mr Gilbert were producing French plays in 1791.

There was nothing so sophisticated on offer from the parish. The two early parochial schools, effectively operating as one, had been joined by a charity school, founded in 1714 for thirty boys and twenty girls from the poor of Hackney. Funded by subscription, and also known as the Blue School from the colour of the free clothes pupils were provided with, the Charity School was based in a house in the churchyard. Both sexes were clothed in blue. The boys had a blue coat with brass buttons, waistcoat, breeches, a cap with a bobble and string and a pair of shoes, while the girls had a blue gown, petticoat, a pair of bodices and buckle shoes. Stockings for boys and girls were knitted by the schoolgirls. Eighteenth-century hours were from 8 a.m. to 12 p.m. and from 2 p.m. to 5 p.m., with Saturday as a half holiday, unless there was a special church service. In 1772 the charity schoolmaster took over the free school and the establishments merged to become the Hackney Free and Charity School. Subscription income was augmented by bequests and charity sermons. Subscribers felt they had rights over pupils and used them for jobs in school time, while local traders supplied the girls with needlework for sale, a practice common to schools of industry and national schools at the time.

In 1804 the Free and Charity School Committee agreed to take children from Stephen Ram's Sunday school (founded in 1726). The extra numbers led the Committee to consider new premises. The vicar, J.J. Watson, took the lead; a piece of land was bought on the east side of Chatham Place and a small classical building with two wings built. Opened in 1811, the new

Hackney Free and Parochial School's second building, Chatham Place, with the New Gravel Pit chapel beyond. Photograph, Alfred Braddock, *c.* 1886.

school had two classrooms, a committee room and living rooms for the master and mistress. Watson also helped found the first infant school in Hackney, which began in premises in Bridge (Ponsford) Street in 1826, moving to a new site on the south side of Paragon Road in 1856. The schools became the Free and Parochial Schools following a bequest in 1842.

Hackney's school of industry was founded in 1790, with a boys' school at Shacklewell and a girls' school at premises in the churchyard, later moved to Jerusalem Square. New premises were opened in Dalston Lane in 1803 for the boys and the girls moved there in 1810, but the school housed only forty girls by 1833. A new building designed by James Edmeston for eighty girls, including the mistress's house, opened on the corner of Dalston Lane and the future Amhurst Road in 1837 and lasted until shortly before 1880. But it was the churches that provided the principal means of cheap education. The Hackney Homerton and Clapton British Schools Association was formed in 1819 and raised funds for a school on Homerton Row. The president was William Hale, who owned a large house and land on the south side of Homerton High Street. The committee was drawn from subscribers paying 10s 6d annually or donated 5 guineas. Children were taught reading, writing and arithmetic and parents paid 1d per week per child. The master's salary was augmented by a percentage of what fees he collected. By 1821 there were 215 children in the school, which had risen to 301 in 1834 with an average attendance of 240. Kingsland and Newington British School was founded in 1808 and by 1848 had 170 day boys and 176 day girls.

The Anglican response had been the formation of national schools, either built on existing foundations or opened as new. Henry Handley Norris, future rector of South Hackney, had

West Hackney Parochial School, as drawn by the architect W. McIntosh Brooks, *c*. 1837.

founded the St John's Chapel School in 1810 in Park Place, Grove Street, with wings for fifty boys and fifty girls flanking rooms for the master and mistress. Norris augmented the funds in 1834 when it became the South Hackney Parochial or Charity School. In 1838 there were 111 boys but only 49 girls and Norris urged local ladies to seek out and send to the school those girls 'who may be living in a state of ignorance and neglect'. When the new church of St John of Jerusalem was built in 1848 the school moved to a new building on Percy Street (now Kingshold Road). West Hackney National Schools were founded in 1829. A school was built on a site donated by W.G. Daniel Tyssen in 1837 for seventy boys and fifty girls.

Both national and British schools faced similar problems. The initial funding had come from subscriptions, augmented by charity sermons, but from the 1830s onwards subscribers diminished and sermons seemed to pull in less funds. There was a recognition that higher teaching standards were needed but good teachers tended to move on quickly. Even when new buildings were put up, funds were not always to hand to finish them before pupils moved in. Girls at West Hackney had to put up with rough brick flooring for a year, during which time the needlework taken in to help school funds was not returned to the traders in the cleanest of conditions. The offer of government grants from the 1840s onwards acted as an incentive to try to ensure that teachers either had or were prepared to sit for teaching certificates, though in the case of female teachers the properly qualified were hard to find, as West Hackney found when it sacked both its unqualified master and mistress in 1847. Certificated teachers also required higher pay. Government inspection could also be critical of school buildings. West Hackney finally established an infant school in 1850 in a rented cottage, which the inspector condemned as being too small and in poor repair in 1862, but despite the threat of the loss of grant for the infants, the committee could not find the funds for a new building and accordingly lost their grant. They were still left with the rental cost of the cottage and the mistress's house, however. In the main school changes were made to desks and a blackboard was introduced in 1854, but additional skylights were beyond their resources. The problem was not resolved until 1873, largely as a result of a generous donation by local High Anglican benefactor Richard Foster. Better buildings could enlarge the intake and either increase the income from pupil fees or else allow weekly rates to be dropped, making it easier for poor children to attend.

Government inspection also encouraged the production of prospectuses. In 1848 children at Kingsland British School were taught arithmetic, geography, English grammar, general and scripture history and lessons in natural science. The girls had the inevitable needlework while some older boys had English composition and drawing. The committee wanted to make what they offered appropriate for the poor but at the same time intended to give the child 'an education that will lift him up in the scale of virtue and intelligence'. In 1854 West Hackney had abandoned taking income from needlework, though girls still had to do it while boys had mechanical science, but both sexes were taught spelling, reading, writing on slates, in copy books and from dictation, arithmetic, geography, grammar and knowledge of common things. Older children did vocal music, outline drawing and natural history. Both national and British schools also had supporting funds for clothing, shoes and help with fees for the poorest households. West Hackney also set up a lending library for the girls with 250 books by 1842.

Other elementary schools in the area included ragged schools, opened at Kingsland in 1848 and Sanford Lane in 1849. There were Wesleyan schools at Homerton and Dalston, a Unitarian school in Chatham Place (established in 1790 by minister Richard Price, which lasted until 1884), and a Roman Catholic school at the Triangle, linked to St John the Baptist church, which opened in 1849.

Hackney's private schools multiplied in the late eighteenth and early nineteenth centuries, though some were short-lived and the quality was very variable. A seller of indecent prints in 1802 did a roaring trade from ladies' schools. One schoolmaster was sued by a parent in 1807 after his son had been beaten for being kept off school following a bite from the master's dog. There were some seventy-one private schools in Hackney in 1826 and some were advertising very widely. In 1828 the Misses Rutherfords were extolling the virtues of their 'Seminary for the Education of Young Ladies' at Upper Clapton in the *Granada Gazette*, claiming it was 'peculiarly eligible for young ladies coming from the West Indies'. The twenty pupils paid 50 guineas per annum basic and 80 guineas for parlour boarders, with 'a native of France resident in the family' and a range of extras, including three languages, use of globes and the harp.

Of considerable national influence was the school at Madras House. This was run by the religious writer John Allen who took in his first pupils in Mare Street in 1817 and moved in 1821 to a larger house on the east side, later no. 208. The school name came from the Madras system of teaching, whereby monitors took responsibility for younger boys, adopted by Allen. Madras House pupils included Edward Steere, future missionary and Bishop of Zanzibar, and Charles Reed, who became Chairman of the London School Board and was knighted. The school passed to Thomas Garland on the death of Allen's son in 1842 and survived under him until after 1879.

Hackney's first grammar school for boys, which also used the Madras system, opened in 1830. The Hackney Proprietary Grammar School, whose proprietors could hold up to three each of the 130 shares, was based in a Gothic-style building at the north-west corner of Sutton Place. Teachers were well paid and although the headmaster was an Anglican, other masters had a nonconformist background. During 1831 a vigorous pamphlet war for and against the school

The Hackney Proprietary Grammar School, Sutton Place. Watercolour by George Hawkins, 1836.

developed locally but more of a problem was the school's selective admissions policy, which excluded the sons of local tradesmen, although the sons of city shopkeepers could become pupils. A rival Church of England Grammar School was launched late in 1829 with links to King's College London, with the rector, J.J. Watson, as president. It was opened in 1830. Its building on the west side of Clarence Road with a Doric portico was designed by William McIntosh Brookes.

Each school had about 120 pupils in the 1830s and there was fierce rivalry between them. Benjamin Clarke was one of the first pupils at the Church of England School and recalled that the rivalry was only resolved when boys from the Charity School attacked Proprietary Grammar schoolboys in the churchyard. The Anglicans

> rushed down Clapton Square, took the path, now by the Coroners' Court, along the Rectory Garden-wall, and outflanked the Charity boys. There really was some military genius shown on the part of our leaders. The fight became fast and furious, stones and other missiles were freely used as well as heavy book straps. In the midst of the combat the police made their appearance and by dropping on the ringleaders (for the Charity boys were the aggressors) the riot was with great difficulty quelled . . .

Numbers at the Proprietary school declined to fifty pupils in 1840 and the schools merged before 1848 on the Clarence Place site. The Sutton Place School became a private house called Sutton Lodge until absorbed into a factory site in the next century. The Church of England School became badly indebted in the late 1870s and after its rescue survived as King's College or Hackney Collegiate School until 1895. It was then closed and the building was sold for a drinks factory before being demolished for the building of flats in 1903.

Other private schools for boys included Wick Hall Collegiate school, based at Wick House in 1841, and run by J.P. Eady and his wife. The prospectus of that year emphasized the practical nature of the curriculum, the healthy surroundings and the watchful care of Mrs Eady:

Hackney Church of England Grammar School. Photograph, Alfred Braddock, *c.* 1890.

in every department – well aired clothing, nothing being allowed to be worn without first undergoing Mrs Eady's inspection – clean warm and judiciously arranged dormitories – frequent personal ablution, every pupil being required to be well washed under proper superintendence, prior to rising from bed and on rising from it – an abundant and unlimited supply of provisions of the best quality, which with the beautiful milk of two fine cows being exclusively applied to the general comfort of the pupils, all form advantages not to be disputed with.

Rear view of Wick Hall Collegiate Hall School, *c.* 1845.

Class in progress at the Clapton School of Art, 1916.

Mrs Eady's solicitude 'alone equalled by the maternal parent herself' was topped off by exercise which included military marching. What the boys thought of it is not recorded. The school was still in operation in 1855, when its curriculum included bookkeeping and its title augmented by the word 'Commercial', but the Wick was shortly to undergo the throes of development and Wick House was empty by 1861, awaiting demolition.

At least sixty-one private schools existed in Hackney in 1861, among them the St John's Foundation School at Clapton House for the sons of poor clergymen (there from 1859 until 1872), whose pupils included Sir Antony Hope Hawkins (the novelist Antony Hope, author of the *Prisoner of Zenda*) and Priory House School, on the west side of Lower Clapton Road. Founded before 1852, the school later moved to Clapton Common and closed in 1909. A former boarding school at no. 81 Clapton Common in the 1880s later became the Clapton and Stamford Hill School of Art from 1888 to 1916, when its LCC grant was withdrawn. Teachers included Florence Bagust, who recorded Hackney's history in words, sketches and photographs.

The City of London was closely involved with three schools that were established or moved to Hackney. The Lady Eleanor Holles School had been founded in 1708. In 1875 funds allowed the construction of a school for middle-class girls and the school opened in a new building, the present no. 182 Mare Street, in 1878. Under the first headmistress, whose increasingly old-fashioned approach had included opposition to a gymnasium as 'unladylike', numbers dropped from a peak of 250 girls to 81 in 1895. But her energetic successor, Ada Beatrice Clark – motto

Hackney Downs School, main building. Photograph, Albert Hester, *c.* 1905.

'straight words, straight deeds and straight backs' – introduced a range of changes. Sport seems to have featured prominently, including gym displays and cricket. Former pupils also recalled the disruption caused by fear of bombing during the First World War when school dinners were taken below desks. Social changes in Hackney in the 1920s resulted in a move to Hampton and the Mare Street School closed in 1935. The building is now part of Cordwainers' College.

Hackney Downs School was founded as a school for middle-class boys in North London by the Grocers' Company. The Company purchased a triangular site on the south side of Hackney Downs in 1872 and the school building, designed by Theophilus Allen, took in its first pupils in September 1876. The first headmaster of the Grocers' Company School was not a success and left after five years, but his replacement, the Revd Charles Gull, made his mark on the school. He introduced science into the curriculum and began a tradition of activity in sport and drama. There was a school battalion, though without uniforms, so children from poorer homes could take part. Gull retired in 1905 before the transfer of the school to the LCC in 1907. Under the LCC the school attracted a wide range of bright pupils, many from Jewish homes, the most famous of whom is probably the playwright Harold Pinter. A major fire destroyed most of the old school buildings in 1963 and while replacements were constructed the school became a comprehensive boys' school. The new buildings opened in 1968. In its later years Hackney Downs School had considerable problems and due to internal disputes within Hackney Council on what action should be taken, the government stepped in and made the school the first in Britain to be taken over by an Education Association. This oversaw the closure of the school in the autumn of 1995.

Skinners' Company opened a girls' school in new premises on nos 111–13 Stamford Hill (later no. 117) in 1890, initially for 250 pupils. The school was voluntary aided from 1949 and by the end of the 1980s the upper school had 290 pupils aged fourteen to nineteen and the lower school 353 aged eleven to thirteen.

Hackney Downs School fife and drum band on the front steps, *c.* 1901.

Hackney has an important place in the history of teaching the deaf. Thomas Braidwood had established the world's first ever school for the deaf in Edinburgh in 1760 and developed a combined system of sign language, speech reading, articulation, reading and writing. It is believed that George III encouraged Braidwood to establish a school for the deaf in London; but for whatever reason Braidwood moved to Hackney in 1783 with his family, who included his daughter Isabella and his nephew John, who had just celebrated a hasty marriage in advance of the birth of their first son Thomas in 1782. Assisted by Joseph Watson the Braidwoods took a lease on Bowling Green House, which they renamed Grove House, reputedly the name of another of Braidwood's nephews, who had been educated among the deaf. He was to become the first headmaster of Britain's first public school for the deaf, which opened in 1792. Braidwood pupils included an illegitimate son of the Whig politician Charles James Fox, about whom the poet Samuel Rogers recalled:

> I once dined at Mr Stone's (at Hackney) with Fox, Sheridan, Talleyrand, Madame de Genlis and some other celebrated persons of the time. A natural son of Fox, a dumb boy (who was the very image of his father) . . . was also there, having come for the occasion from Braidwood's Academy. To him, Fox almost entirely confined his attentions, conversing with him by fingers; and their eyes glistened as they looked at each other. Talleyrand remarked to me 'How strange it was, to dine in company with the finest Orator in Europe and only to see him talk with his fingers!'

Miss Crogham addresses a class with partial hearing at the Homerton School for the Deaf, 1904.

The academy moved from Grove House to Pembroke House on the west side of Mare Street in 1799. Thomas Braidwood senior retired in that year and died at the Grove Street house in 1806 aged ninety-one; he was buried in St Thomas Square chapel burial ground. John Braidwood left in 1809 for Scotland and ultimately America and Thomas went to Birmingham in 1814. Isabella was left to run the Academy, which moved from Pembroke House in 1810 to a house near Cambridge Heath until 1813, when the Hackney connection was finally broken.

The London County Council had a day school for the deaf in Homerton Row in 1899 and the following year made use of the former premises of Homerton College as a residential school for the deaf and deaf and blind. Under the energetic guidance of Frank Barnes, activities included holidays at Osea Island on the Essex coast and at New Romney, where the teachers used sheep, fish and animal life for counting and the little children did sand-writing or filling in the shapes of words with stones. Barnes was also a Church of England lay reader and the congregation for his services came from the Dr Barnardo's Home for Deaf Children in Mare Street and the Asylum for Deaf and Dumb Women at Clapton. The Homerton school moved to Penn in Buckinghamshire in 1921.

Parliamentary grants helped improve some Hackney schools and thirteen establishments received grants in 1871, including the London Orphan Asylum, the Dalston and Elizabeth Fry refuges and the Tre-Wint Industrial Home. Under the Education Act of 1870 a division of the London School Board was created for Hackney and Bethnal Green, which took over the Kingsland and Shacklewell ragged school when its managers threatened closure, and the majority of its seven Hackney schools in 1873 were existing foundations. There was the possibility of competition with successful national schools, which became actual when the vicar of St Michael's went ahead with a large new national school near the Board school in Lamb Lane, though the Board's proposal to build a new school opposite the Free and Parochial School in Chatham Place was defeated in 1875.

School attendance was just one of the problems the Board faced and attempted to solve by setting up a special school. The old Ryder House on Upper Homerton (later Urswick Road) opened as an industrial school in 1878 to avoid legal difficulties around detentions, although in practice it was a truant school from its inception. The old house was demolished in 1885 and the new school held 100 boys. Boys were taught tailoring, shoemaking, gardening, laundry work, metalwork and industrial drawing and the fourteen-hour day included drill and gymnastics. The majority of boys spent three months there. The school closed in 1913, though the premises were used as an open-air school for 130 delicate children from 1928 to about 1940.

Despite being thought extravagant, the Board had opened thirteen permanent schools by 1880 and added a further six in the ensuing ten years. Four national schools closed and of four nonconformist schools receiving grants, only one, Dalston Wesleyan, survived in 1903. Of all the Church of England schools, only the Hackney Free and Parochial managed to grow to the size of a board school. Government inspections from 1864 onwards had helped raise standards but in 1893 the inspectors condemned the three basement classrooms in the Chatham Place building. The rector took the lead in raising funds for a new school. The purchase of Sutton House by Algernon Lawley for use as the St John's Church Institute provided land and the garden became the site for the Isabella Road School, which opened in 1896. The Chatham Place building was sold in the following year and survived in industrial use until its demolition in 1973.

The Isabella Road building was rebuilt in 1937 and a fourth school was added to the governors' responsibilities, when Ram's Episcopal chapel was closed in 1937, in the shape of Ram's Infants' School. During the Second World War the infant school in Paragon Road was bomb-damaged, Ram's was requisitioned and conditions at Isabella Road left much to be desired. The governors decided to demolish the Paragon Road site and build a new secondary school on the extended site (enlarged again in 1963). Isabella Road School was refurbished for junior mixed, while a new infants' school to the south-west allowed the Ram's site to be abandoned. A further series of changes were implemented from 1993, when the secondary school was enlarged again, allowing the closure of an overflow site on Lansdowne Drive. The junior and infants' schools were merged to create a new school, Ram's Episcopal Primary School.

The London School Board was abolished in 1903. It had provided Hackney with twenty-eight schools and places for 33,435 pupils. The new education committee of the LCC which succeeded the LSB in 1904 had added three secondary schools by 1909: Hackney Downs from the Grocers' Company, Colvestone Crescent (the former Kingsland Birkbeck School, founded under the auspices of William Ellis in 1852 for middle-class children and taken over by the LCC in 1905) and Cassland Road. Three central schools were opened between 1910 and 1913 at Lauriston Road, Millfields Road and Wilton Road. Three Anglican and two Roman Catholic schools survived the Second World War, along with twenty-three county primary schools, sixteen county secondary schools and a county nursery school in 1951. Under the London Government Act of 1963 Hackney became a division of ILEA in 1965 and there were fifty primary schools and a Jewish voluntary school when ILEA was abolished in 1990. Hackney's own education authority had amalgamated six junior and infant schools by 1993 but also faced increasing criticism over its handling of local education and the gap following the resignation of its first education director. A programme of change is to be implemented following the appointment of a new director in 1998.

6. BUSINESS & INDUSTRY

One of the earliest references to business enterprise in Hackney comes in 1377, when local hucksters – the medieval equivalent of market traders – selling cheese in London, were accused of buying it up at source in order to sell it at a better profit: described in the speech of the time as 'regrating'. Sixteenth-century trades recorded locally included embroiderers, joiners and sawyers and in the following century, moniers (probably money lenders), victuallers and vintners.

Hackney's earliest industrial buildings were its mills. The Templars built a watermill on the Leyton side of their Hackney and Leyton land after 1185 and by 1307 there was a second mill on the Hackney side, giving Temple Mills its name. The main mill was used to grind corn but the other was used from the sixteenth century for a variety of industries – a leather mill before 1593 was succeeded by a powder mill, which had given way to another process by 1627. Prince Rupert used a watermill on Hackney Marsh, possibly at Temple Mills, to make 'prince's metal' for guns to a special formula he is said to have taken to his grave in 1682. A company formed in 1695 made brass, tin and tin utensils, and was close to bankruptcy and the subject of a dispute in 1721. After a lapse of some years, sheet lead was made at the mills from about 1757 to after 1814.

Mill Fields take their name from a mill extant in 1381 which may have been a watermill, but would appear to have gone by the seventeenth century. Water also played an important part in another early Hackney industry. The premises to the west of Sutton House were known as the Tan House in the sixteenth century, from a tannery in operation in the previous century.

The mills at Lea Bridge had their origin in a project to supply Hackney with piped water. Lord of the manor Francis Tyssen II had acquired substantial property holdings in the parish after 1697, including land at Jeremy's Ferry, north of the present Lea Bridge. Tyssen was an East India merchant and had been involved in a number of early joint stock companies, including the Hampstead Aqueduct Company, floated in 1692 to supply London with water. Tyssen set up a waterworks at the weir at Jeremy's Ferry between 1707 and 1709, with an engine, possibly a waterwheel, to raise water from the river. Pipes or a wooden conduit carried it to a reservoir at Clapton and it would have been distributed to households by wooden pipes. By 1715 there was a resident engineer, Randolph Johnson. But after the death of Tyssen's son in 1717, the works were allowed to fall into disrepair. The speculator John Ward, representing Tyssen's infant son, proposed to repair and expand the works in 1724, introducing a cast-iron engine. But Ward was already in financial difficulties and shortly after his proposal he was convicted of forgery. The works ceased to function and local householders had to fall back on wells, pumps, rainwater, or, as Parliament was told in 1762, 'by Carts from the River, which is very expensive'. The reservoir remained at Clapton but it was now just a pond, no longer supplied from the Lea.

Lea Bridge mills, a watercolour by C. Bigot, *c*. 1830.

The residents might have accepted the situation but in the mid-eighteenth century Hackney was a popular resort in the summer for visitors. In April 1755 a newspaper noted that 'many persons who last year had summer lodgings at Hackney and Homerton are determined to go elsewhere this year on account of the scarcity of soft water in those villages: 'tis a pity the opulent inhabitants . . . do not remove the cause of this complaint . . . by laying the new River Water'. Unfortunately, when an approach was made to the New River Company in 1757, the parish could not guarantee the company a minimum annual income of £250 and negotiations fell through.

It was not until 1760 that a fresh effort was made. In that year Francis John Tyssen granted a lease to John Barrow and Thomas and Henry Holloway of land just south of Lea Bridge to establish a waterworks for Hackney. The new venture also took on Chevaliers Ferry House on the east side of the river two years later and was financed by share capital. The works were new but utilized some of the pipework of the old scheme and the reservoir at Clapton; a new cut was built alongside the Lea and over it were built mills to raise water and grind corn. A tower was built on the west bank, presumably to raise pressure for the supply.

The new channel to the mill required locks across the Lea and led to complaints from bargemen to the trustees of the Lea Navigation. Eventually the matter was resolved when the trustees took over the locks and appointed a lock-keeper to ensure balanced use between barges and waterworks. The Hackney Cut was constructed in 1769, leaving the Lea just above the mills, and going though the marsh east of Hackney Wick. The mills, of brick and timber, were in the hands of partners Jonathan Rogers and Charles Hammerton in 1776, but a series of millers and mealmen conducted their business there. Jonathan Roger's successor, Richard Rogers, was bankrupted in 1790 but Hamerton & Co. carried on. There were other businesses using the premises, including an enterprise grinding needle points run by the appropriately named Messrs Sharpe (which had been started in 1783 at Temple Mills). The mills and the needle factory were burnt down in January 1796 but later rebuilt. Hamerton's interests were sold out and John Killick became the miller, surviving a bankruptcy in 1809. In the 1820s the waterworks attracted the attention of larger concerns, principally the East London Waterworks Company, one of whose directors was the influential Hackney resident Richard Dann. Killick's bankruptcy appears to have cost him the lease, which was in the hands of the Surrey brothers, but it was close to its expiry date and the Tyssens, who still owned the freehold, had no intention of renewing it. In the event it was Killick who got a new lease in 1820 and repaired the mills. Killick expressed interest in selling out to the East London Company but the parties were unable to come to an agreement.

It was legal pressure on the East London Company that forced them to acquire the Hackney works. A Royal Commission of 1828 showed concern that they were taking drinking water from below the tidal limit of the polluted Thames. So in 1829 the company introduced a bill to take water from the Lea above the mills. In the face of objections from Killick and the Tyssens, agreement was eventually arrived at in 1830–2 for the purchase of Killick's lease and the Tyssens' freehold interest. The flour mills were pulled down in 1833 and by the following year a new canal had been completed just to the east of the Hackney Cut to take water down to the reservoirs at Old Ford, though filter beds were not constructed there for another thirty-three years. However Clapton Pond ceased to be a reservoir at this time and the Hackney supply was taken straight from the river. In 1837 new waterworks at Lea Bridge were linked to a settling reservoir at Stamford Hill.

Hackney's other mills were purpose-built industrial premises, although some were to go through a variety of uses. Joseph Barbaroux's sale of the Wick House estate in 1763 led to the construction of a mill and house on the main channel of the Hackney Brook to the north-east of Wick House for Messrs Turners, papermakers. The mill had a thirteen-foot diameter wheel with double arms, while the works were equipped with an oak press for pressing paper; iron-bound backs and vats, and embossing presses were among other effects. But the enterprise lasted barely two years before being sold up in 1765. Successor businesses included Samuel Froggatt's optical glassworks established in 1821 and still flourishing in 1849. The mill buildings were probably demolished in the mid-1860s, since part of the tail race of the mill stream was still extant on the 1870 Ordnance Survey map.

There were silkweavers at Hackney in 1609. The parish supplied an old silkweaver with a loom in 1659 but the trade had probably died out locally by the time Leny Smith leased a mill in 1787 to use for his silk business. The mill had once been used for fulling and subsequently by William Smith (no relation) as a tobacco and snuff mill. Leny Smith established a London office in 1791 and by 1811 he and his son were the largest silk producers in the country, employing a mostly female workforce of 600 to 700 people at the Hackney Wick mill and at Taunton in Somerset. The mill lay just south of Hackney Brook on a site south-west of the junction of the present Wick and Cassland roads, and was originally powered with water diverted from the brook into its own millpond, although two steam engines were later introduced. The works prepared silk from the raw state for the loom and also dressed and finished it for the weaver. Some of his workforce were casuals – or claimed as such for tax purposes – but prior to 1814 four workers' cottages had been constructed along Silk Mill Row, later the northern part of Cassland Road, and Bakers Row cottages on the north side of what is now Victoria Park Road, which Smith rebuilt in 1822. Smith had a house built for himself and his family to the north of the mill in 1808–9 (later Sidney House and now part of the Convent of the Sacred Heart). But

Leny Smith's mill, *c.* 1830.

the silk trade declined and by 1828 the mill was idle and Smith's house and business in the hands of his mortgagees. The mill was later to be used by Captain Edward Brenton's Children's Friend Society to prepare children for emigration to the colonies. By 1840 the millpond was stagnant and overloaded with sewage from the cottages in Silk Mill Row, while adjoining well water was also polluted. Both were said to be a contributing factor to the deaths of two infants in the cottages in 1840 by the visiting doctor, the future antiquarian Benjamin Clarke. Perhaps the quality of the water was a factor in the demise of Brenton's Asylum, which vacated the former factory in 1842. It last saw use as a flock and horsehair factory before being demolished for redevelopment by 1849.

Two other industrial concerns made good use of the waters of the Hackney Brook, both in the vicinity of the present Ponsford Street. This was once Bridge Street, named from the Blew Bridge over the brook, linking Homerton to Morning Lane and in existence before 1657. To the west of it was the Woolpack brewery, which took its name from a nearby inn, first licensed in 1760. Owned by the Addison family from the early 1800s, it was demolished in 1850 for the construction of the North London Railway, although the Addison house to the north of the railway survived into the twentieth century.

While brook water went into the beer west of the bridge, it emerged further downstream iridescent with colours. In 1760 a German immigrant, Lewis Steigenberger, who had changed his name to Berger, established a works for making Prussian blue at Shadwell. In 1780 he moved his colour manufactury from there to Homerton, renting a farmhouse on Shepherds Lane with a field at the rear with its own well. Berger rebuilt the house and established a factory for dry colours and later paint at the southern end of the field on to Morning Lane. The brook was diverted through the

Workmen pose outside the loading area at Lewis Berger & Sons' Homerton factory, *c.* 1870.

grounds to provide ornamental water and essential water for the factory, although the diversion also reduced flooding to the south in Morning Lane (that section being known as Water Lane).

The Homerton factory enabled Berger to manufacture more colours and he began to experiment with pigments ground in oil. Lewis Berger died in 1814 but his sons and grandsons gradually expanded the business. The company had city offices in Well Court, while one of Lewis's sons, John, owned the hall on the former Hackney House estate and the other, Samuel, lived nearby. For many years the factory kept a rather rural appearance, retaining a pasture – cut through by the viaduct of the North London line but used for occasional cricket matches – an old dairy, cottages and stables. But from the 1870s the site became more industrial and the ornamental waters, former farm buildings and all but a small area of lawn at the back of Lewis's former house were built over. The clock tower originally erected in 1805 was salvaged and set above one of the new warehouses, while the Hackney Brook was eventually culverted in 1870. There were about eighty employees at Hackney and probably another twenty in the city offices at Well Court. Some workers remained with the company for life; others were sacked for offences that included drunkeness, foul language, fighting 'and refusing to work in the Blue Place' – presumably one of the more unpleasant places in the factory.

After the death of Samuel Berger in 1855 and his brother John five years later the business passed to Capel B. Berger and Lewis C. Berger. In 1879 they turned Lewis Berger & Sons into a limited company. The new managing director was a member of the next generation, Arthur John Berger, but his period of control was to prove disastrous. Unwise investment in a Sheffield leadworks proved a poor start and an enormous outlay on new buildings at Homerton in the early 1890s made matters worse. A new assistant manager, John Garson, appointed in 1894, discovered that Arthur Berger had been taking money from the company for his own private affairs. Berger was finally removed in 1895 but poor trading nearly resulted in the liquidation of Bergers in 1902. Eventually the company was sold to an American concern, Sherwin Williams, in 1905. Industrial sickness led to a strike at the factory in 1911 but the management stood firm and the workforce had to return to what their representatives described as 'the sheds of death'. The Berger business grew in the 1920s and the plant survived bomb damage to the varnish works in the Second World War. Paint manufacture finally ended at Homerton in 1960.

Calico printing and dyeing also needed water and by 1774 there was a large calico factory at Spring Hill, occupied by George Baker's dyeworks and William Burch's calico-printing works. The works were still there in 1855, making use of what was later known as Giles Dock, which ran parallel from the Lea alongside Spring Hill. The works were sited on Spring Lane in 1831 but by 1870 all traces of industry except the dock had gone. The whole site now forms part of Springfield Park. William Connell had a bleaching and dyeing business at the Lea Valley works at Baker's Hill which lasted until taken over in 1960, and John Hammond had a calico-printing works just to the south of Lea Dock in 1832.

Brick-making and gravel extraction were taking place at Clapton in the early sixteenth century; crofts called Brickhill and the Gravel Pit were recorded there in 1535. Bricks for Ralph Sadleir's 'bryk place' (today's Sutton House), built during 1534–5, would have been made locally. Bricks were being made on land south of Balmes House in 1631, when a complaint by Sir George Whitmore stopped the activity, though after the Civil War, in 1660, the Whitmores leased land just south of their house for brick-making. By 1756 the Balmes estate included three fields called the Further, Middle and Hither brickfields. Bricks were being made on land east of

High Bridge with tile kiln, a watercolour attributed to C. Bigot, c. 1815. The calico drying ground lay just to the south of the kiln.

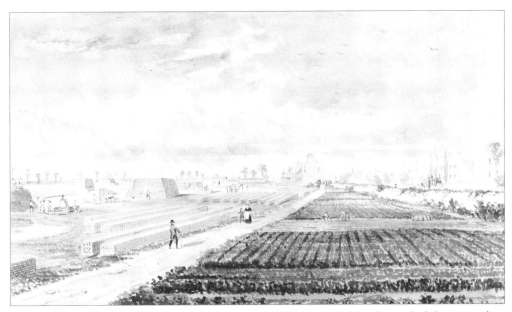

Brick-making on the future De Beauvoir Town estate, *c.* 1825. Kingsland Road is on the left. Watercolour by C.H. Matthews, *c.* 1850.

Mare Street in 1704 and north of Dalston Lane in 1706. Bricks and tiles were made in large quantities around Kingsland by 1795 and by 1806 brickfields occupied 170 acres of land in Hackney – more than market gardens and nurseries. Although local brick-earth was to be used in the successive house building periods in the nineteenth century, there were insufficient materials to meet demand for the building of De Beauvoir Town and supplies were brought in via the Kingsland wharf. Clapton was a centre of brick-making in the 1840s and many of the eleven victims of a boating accident on the Lea in September 1840 were the sons of brick-making families living in Caroline and Brook Streets, Clapton. The last of Hackney's brickfields was probably the one just to the north of Lea Dock, which was still in use in 1883 but had gone by 1901. Gravel digging for road repair also had a long local history and the pits to the south of Morning Lane, which were to give their name to the Gravel Pit chapel, were already old in 1697.

From the mid-nineteenth century many industries were attracted to Hackney Wick: raw materials could be brought in by water, waste disposed of, and the railway line and the Hackney Cut provided a barrier of sorts from the better-off parts of Hackney. The first plastic in Britain, parkesine, was produced by inventor Alexander Parkes in Wallis Road in 1862. The process was taken over by Daniel Spill in 1869, who traded as the Xylonite Company, but he too went bankrupt in 1874. Spill moved to no. 124 Homerton High Street in 1875 and two years later combined with his neighbour, L.P. Merriam, who had tried to promote celluloid, the American equivalent of Xylonite. The British Xylonite Company went on to become a major plastics manufacturer of products, which included 'cuffs, collars, and fronts', as well as mock tortoiseshell items. The stiff plastic collars and cuffs were to become popular around the turn of the century and sold very well. Sheet production moved to Brantham in Suffolk in 1887 and the Homerton site was sold when the company moved its remaining operations to Hale End, Walthamstow, in 1897.

Daniel Spill's Ivoride works on the south side of Homerton High Street, *c.* 1880. The main building fronting on to the High Street appears rather grander and Macintosh Lane in front much wider than either was in actuality.

Other factories at Hackney Wick included James Ingram's vulcanized rubber works, which had moved from Hoxton in 1866 to a site on the east side of Chapman Road. There was an ironworks on Wallis Road, a ropery on the site of the present St Mary at Eton church and a tar and chemical works beyond Wick Lane Bridge, all established before 1870. The Atlas Works on Gainsborough Road were used for the manufacture of aniline dyes by Brooke, Simpson and Spiller by 1875. Achille Serre came to England as a refugee after the Franco-Prussian War and established one of Britain's earliest dry-cleaning businesses in Carpenters Road in 1877. Eugene Carless established his distilling and oil refining business in 1859 on land adjoining White Post Lane, building the Hope Chemical Works. Partnership with John Hare Leonard led to the creation of Carless Capel and Leonard, who expanded the business and by the mid-1890s were importing a range of products, including petroleum spirit. An associate of Gottlieb Daimler, Frederick Sims, suggested a catchier name and the brand name 'petrol' was born. To the north of the Wick were the extensive works of Clarke Nickolls and Coombs, confectionery makers, established in 1872, one of the first British companies to introduce a profit-sharing scheme for its employees. The company remained Hackney based until about 1975. Hackney Wick was a small place and many of these businessmen would have known each other: the area has been described as a nineteenth-century science park by one industrial historian.

Elsewhere in Hackney industrial concerns were smaller but employed an increasing proportion of the local workforce. There were already furniture firms in Hackney in the 1890s, as the industry spread north from Shoreditch and Bethnal Green. They occupied premises east of Mare Street, adjoining the Great Eastern Railway line, and near the North London Railway south of Homerton High Street. By 1901 there were over 5,000 employed as cabinet-makers

Barges alongside Latham's wharf, north of Lea Bridge.

and in associated trades, including piano-making. Some of the fourteen Hackney firms listed in 1880 did not survive into the next century but in 1924 Hackney's piano-makers included Broadwood White & Co. Innovative furniture-makers included Greaves and Thomas, founded in 1905, who moved to Northwold Road in 1911. They introduced a range of dual-purpose furniture, including a convertible 'Put-U-Up' settee-bed in 1922. The firm left Hackney in about 1965. Some of the wood required by the furniture trade would have come through James Latham's warehouses alongside Middlesex Wharf, established in 1912. Latham's had moved from Liverpool to Shoreditch in 1815 and gradually expanded their works at Middlesex Wharf, which by 1960 incorporated an extensive tramway system, with timber sheds surrounding the King's Head public house.

Clothing and footwear makers employed a further 15,000 people in 1901. Many of these were women, working as dressmakers, shirtmakers, seamstresses and milliners. Large tailoring firms included Simeon Simpson, who had begun as a city tailor in 1894. Simpson's son expanded the business and built a model factory at nos 92–100 Stoke Newington Road in 1929. The company created the Daks range of clothing in 1934 and survived war damage to continue manufacturing in Hackney until about 1982. Their building is now the Halkevi Turkish Community Centre. Other firms included Gerrish Ames and Simpkins, founded in Basingstoke in 1878, who bought the redundant Morley Hall at the Triangle during the First World War; Moss Brothers (who had a workshop south of Balls Pond Road in 1961); and the firm of Alfred Polikoff. Polikoff had a factory at London Lane by 1915 and then moved to a new building at nos 148–50 Mare Street. This burned down in a spectacular fire in 1932 and the company moved to a new factory on the west side of Chatham Place. This was also war-damaged and by

1952 was shared by Burberrys. Both companies were taken over by Great Universal Stores. The Polikoff name disappeared but Burberrys remain at nos 29–53 Chatham Place, visited now by tourists from as far afield as Japan. Horne Brothers, the makers of men's clothes, opened a new factory on the north side of King Edward's Road in 1922. In 1948 they claimed that their factory's spaciousness and employee benefits were admired throughout the trade. Horne's left in 1987 and Durigo House was later used for document storage.

The boot and shoe trade also moved north. As early as 1880 there was a concentration of the industry in Ash Grove and Mentmore Terrace, and thirty-eight of the forty-three listed North London firms were Hackney based. Lax enforcement by St Thomas Hospital of the leasing covenants of its Well Street properties allowed bootmaking businesses to establish themselves in the terrace houses there from 1884. Within the decade seventeen businesses were based there. By 1938 Hackney was the centre of the London footwear trade, with many Jewish-run businesses. Eleazer Phillips took over the former YMCA at nos 273–5 Mare Street (built as private houses in 1838) and claimed in 1948 to be the oldest shoe factory in Hackney, employing 200 people making the 'Betta' and 'Sunray' range of shoes. Well Street has retained its associations with the shoe trade, although many other firms, including Phillips, have left the area.

In common with many areas of London, Hackney had its own local printers from the 1830s onwards. Caleb Turner published a local almanac in 1842 and went on to produce Hackney's first home-grown directory of local businesses in 1843. In common with many other printers Turner was a radical. He opposed the compulsory church rate levied on all local inhabitants – whether Anglicans or not – before 1866 and he crossed the path of Hackney's vestry clerk Charles Horton Pulley. Turner claimed in a pamphlet that Pulley had threatened him with horsewhipping at one point! Turner's directories were continued by Messrs Green and Simpson in the late 1860s but the comprehensive local street and trade directories of the mid-1880s to the late 1920s were the work of the London-wide firm Kellys. On a bigger scale Eyre and Spottiswoode set up a factory at Shacklewell to print bibles in about 1829 and remained there until about 1936. Reeves and Sons moved their artists' colour factory from the city to a new building on the site of the Luxembourg Hall in Ashwin Street in 1866. Reeves's decorated building survived war damage and although the firm left in the mid-1950s, their refurbished factory has provided a home to a range of projects including Bootstrap Enterprises, a community employment project.

Hackney's first news magazine was the *Hackney Magazine and Parish Reformer*. This was published by another of Hackney's early printers, Charles Green, who mixed historical features with strong advocacy for more open local government. The *Shoreditch Observer*, founded in 1857, also circulated in Hackney and incorporated the name *Hackney Express* in its title after 1868. It closed in 1915. There was a range of other short-lived titles but Hackney's most successful paper remains the *Hackney Gazette*, which broadly supported the Liberal and Radical interests. Founded in 1864, and mainly supported by volunteers at first, the *Gazette* soon passed to printer Charles Potter. Operating from offices at no. 440 Kingsland Road, with a small printing works, the Lenthall works, on the corner of Richmond and Glebe Roads, the *Gazette* moved to the more spacious no. 505a Kingsland Road in 1924, to 250–256 Kingsland Road in Shoreditch in 1958, and is now based in Bethnal Green. The Potter family sold their interests in the mid-1980s and today's *Gazette* has achieved national prominence through its fictional counterpart, the *Walford Gazette* of BBC's *EastEnders*. In the mid-1880s two rivals were founded for the local market, the *Hackney Mercury*, which broadly supported the Conservatives, and the

North London Guardian, but neither stayed the course. The *Mercury* closed in 1910 and the *North London Guardian*, in its final incarnation as the *Stoke Newington and Hackney Chronicle,* was absorbed by the *Gazette* in 1971. There were a number of radical alternative papers founded in the late 1960s; the longest running of these, the *Hackney People's Paper*, closed in 1984.

Hackney has also been home to more diverse businesses. Tyer & Co., who made railway signalling equipment in Ashwin Street up to the mid-1960s, originated locally. The antiquarian Benjamin Clarke hosted a demonstration in his dining room of the block system from their young founder in the 1850s. Other electrical and engineering firms included Siemens Brothers, who made electrical lamps at a Dalston factory from 1908 to 1924, and the Marconi Wireless Telegraph Company at Tyssen Street from 1905. From 1915, and for the duration of the First World War, the War Department's National Projectile factory made munitions near the Hackney Cut. E.C. Barlow & Sons moved from Shoreditch to Urswick Road by 1903 and from 1929 formed a branch of the Metal Box Company. Their works included the former Hackney Proprietary Grammar School at the west end of Sutton Place, demolished in 1959 when a new factory was built on the site. The majority of the works were demolished after Metal Box moved out in about 1983 and Sutton Square now stands on the site. The Mentmore Manufacturing Company began making fountain pens from no. 16 Mentmore Terrace in 1921. The firm moved to Tudor Grove two years later and by 1948 claimed to be the largest fountain pen maker in Europe, famous for its Platignum brand. The firm of J.G. Franklin, founded in Hoxton in 1864 to make surgical goods from rubber and celluloid, moved to the Birkbeck Road by 1893, later expanding into the Birkbeck Works on Colveston Crescent. By 1948 it was employing 500 people making a range of surgical goods. Their telegraphic address in the mid-1950s was 'Expanding Hackney'. The company moved to Lea Bridge Road in 1974 and was last listed in London directories in the following year. The Venus Pencil Company was based at nos 169–71 Lower Clapton Road from 1903 until shortly before 1970.

Local industry had its sweeter side. Besides confectioners Clarnicos, W.J. Bush were the first English firm to make flavour essences and had moved from their original city factory to Ash Grove by 1880. From their Grove works they issued culinary goods to promote their range and maintained a Hackney presence until about 1973; at this point the works closed and the site was redeveloped as a new bus garage. In 1894 the Crown Perfumery moved to a new factory on the east side of Kenworthy Road (then Sidney Road) and stretching back along Tynte Street. The business had grown from the Thomson family business of corset-making. One son had been intrigued by female conversations in the company showrooms about perfumes and one early company product, smelling salts, would have had a practical use in the fitting room if the corset proved to be too tight for the customer. The Crown Perfumery was established in 1872 as an associated business and after the move to Hackney offered soaps, bath salts, colognes and even cherry toothpaste. By 1900 there were Crown factories in Austria, Denmark, France and Germany and the company was one of the largest of its kind in Europe. So pervasive were the odours round Kenworthy Road that the locals referred to working 'up the scent'. The Thomsons sold the business to soap-makers William Gossage in 1921 and two years later the Hackney factory closed.

Most Hackney firms who suffered bomb damage rebuilt their factories. Perhaps the greatest postwar success story was Lesney Products, founded by Leslie Smith and John Odell in 1947, as pressure dyecasters. Lesney moved to 1a Shacklewell Lane in 1950 but Smith & Odell's business received a boost when they made a detailed model of the Coronation coach in 1953. At just over an inch long, this model went on to sell over a million. In the same year

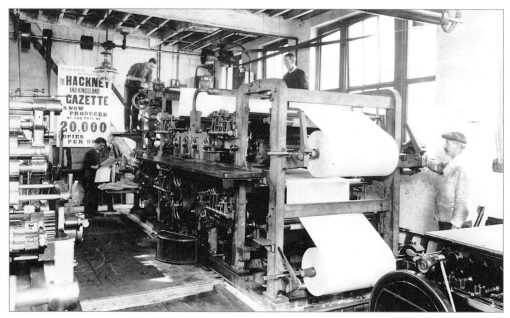

The new rotary printing press at the Hackney Gazette's works, *c.* 1925.

they began making the Matchbox model vehicles, selling at 1*s* 6*d* each, and demand was such that the company moved twice, first to Eastway in 1959 and then to a large new factory between Lee Conservancy Road and the Hackney Cut in 1975. Lesney became a public company in 1960 and by 1982 the company was probably Hackney's largest business employer, with 1,500 employees. But in the following year competition from the toy market abroad forced the firm into liquidation. The company was acquired by a Hong Kong based group and the range revived but the Hackney factory stood empty for over ten years before being converted to flats.

The movement of large firms out of Hackney was part of the general progression of manufacturing businesses out of inner London, but what began in the 1960s, accelerated in the 1970s, and was made worse by the recession of the early 1980s. Large factories were either demolished or subdivided among smaller firms and in the 1990s Burberrys is one of the comparatively few large-scale manufacturing employers to remain, although the clothing and shoe trade remain important and there are a wide range of smaller firms.

By 1826 there was a varied range of shops in Church Street, Mare Street, Well Street, Homerton, Clapton and Kingsland. These included thirty butchers, thirty-six grocers and forty-two carpenters. Miscellaneous trades included two perfumers on Church Street, seven toy shops and stationers (two of whom also ran libraries), two booksellers (one of whom ran a circulating library) and four wine merchants. Church Street and Kingsland included a number of glass and china dealers and haberdashers, though the bulk of the linen drapers were all on Church Street. William Holmes's business was to become Green and Branscombe's just south of the railway bridge, later nos 333–5 Mare Street, whose site forms part of the Hackney branch of Woolworths, established there in 1922. Matthew Rose took over an existing business at London House, Church Street, in 1852. He took over adjoining

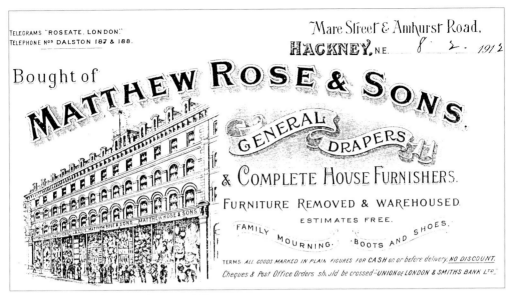

Bill head from Matthew Rose's store, 1912.

shops and expanded south to provide a shop front on Amhurst Road in 1868. The widening of the former Church Street (then Mare Street) in 1877 enabled Rose to expand further south, so that by 1900 Rose's was Hackney's principle department store, selling furniture, glass, china, ironmongery and even having a removals service. Rose's closed in 1936 and the majority of the site was acquired by Marks and Spencers. Henry Spokes built up a draper's business from no. 5 Lower Clapton Road in 1894, expanding in the 1930s to take in nos 1–17 but closing in 1966. T.B. Stephens, who began as a draper in 1904, built a three-storey department store at nos 230–40 Stoke Newington High Street, which survived until about 1973. Among Hackney's longest serving businesses today is the cash furnishing business, effectively established by Elizabeth Gibbons in nos 1–17 Amhurst Road, and dating from the 1890s. Cooke's eel and pie business founded in Shoreditch opened a branch at no. 41 Kingsland High Street in 1910 and became something of a tourist attraction, but closed on the retirement of the owners in 1997. The building has been listed and the façade and shop fittings have been retained by the Chinese restaurant that now occupies the shop.

Hackney had no traditional markets though by 1893 street markets existed in Kingsland Road, Mare Street, Well Street and in the Broadway, London Fields. There was a shellfish seller's barrow outside Hackney station and stallholders selling plants and other goods just south of the railway bridge, but Mare Street's market had ceased by the 1930s. The Kingsland Road market moved north, first to Kingsland High Street and then by 1930 to Ridley Road, where today it provides fruit and vegetable stalls at the west end and a diverse range of goods further east. A successor market remained on the east side of Kingsland Road between Richmond and Middleton Roads, known as the Waste, with a range of stalls selling vegetables, shoes, clothing and household goods. Chatsworth Road, which was the largest of Hackney's street markets in the 1890s, had over 200 licensed pitches in the 1930s but the market declined in the early 1990s and closed altogether in 1997.

7. Victorian Hackney

The seventy years from 1830 saw the transformation of Hackney from a series of linear villages separated by open fields to an inner London suburb. The map of the parish produced in 1831 shows the outlines of the Rhodes grand development for De Beauvoir Town and the new Richmond Road running east from Kingsland Road, all but empty of housing. The Rhodes scheme for a new district for De Beauvoir Town was defeated by Richard Benyon de Beauvoir, but Rhodes and other Dalston landowners produced a grid pattern of streets for the area between Kingsland Road, London Fields and Willow Walk, and building was under way in the late 1830s and 1840s. Cooperation between landowners also took place in South Hackney, where leases on the Cass and Norris estates granted in the 1780s came to an end in the 1840s. The Cass surveyor, George Wales, and the Norris estate surveyor, Henry Currey, were able to arrange exchanges of land to make road planning on both estates easier. South Hackney was largely built up by 1870. Some building had been carried out by developers making piecemeal purchases and in some cases the resulting houses ended up at the lower end of the social scale. William Bradshaw, who had also built parts of Hackney Wick, was responsible for Morpeth Road in South Hackney, one of the poorest streets in the area by the 1890s.

Hackney village began to take on an urban look with the construction of the railway bridge in 1850 and the culverting of Hackney Brook in 1859–60. In 1866 a major road junction was created by the development of Amhurst Road across the former Spurstowe estate, and terraces to the south had been completed by 1870. After the completion of the Great Eastern railway line in 1872, building spread west of Mare Street. The watercress beds just south of the North London Railway viaduct were built over in 1875 (and now form the site of Tesco's supermarket). Two major road-widening schemes completed the transformation – 250 yards of the west side of the former Church Street, north of the bridge, was demolished in 1877–9 and, after much debate, Mare Street from the Triangle to the bridge were widened in stages between 1902 and 1906. Hackney's first council housing was put up on Valette Street as part of

Mare Street transformed – a view north from the King's Head public house to the new North London railway bridge. Lithograph, 1853.

London County Council housing in Valette Street, seen shortly after completion in 1904.

a clearance that replaced Jerusalem Square and Passage in 1902, Valette Buildings being completed in 1906.

Dalston was described as 'a recently increased suburban village with some handsome old houses' in 1849. The Massie family, who had inherited the Graham estate, planned a development as early as 1853, which included the western end of Graham Road, Alma (later Ritson) Road and the west side of Fasset Square, though the last two were not finished until the late 1860s. Graham Road was not completed through to Mare Street until the early 1870s, though by 1870 there were houses all the way along Dalston Lane and Amhurst Road east between Dalston and Hackney village. By the early 1880s most of Dalston and Kingsland had been built over, with the remains of Kingsland Green lined up for development in 1882, despite local protests. By 1890 Queens Road, Parkholme Road and parts of Richmond and Forest Roads were well-to-do, although there were pockets of poverty south of Wilman Grove and behind Kingsland High Street. De Beauvoir Town was mostly built up by the mid-1850s and was intended to be wholly residential, except for the area round Kingsland Basin off the Regent's Canal, itself completed in 1823. But the area declined socially from the 1880s – arguably the Rhodes proposals for greater density in the area north of Downham Road would have made more economic sense, though they would probably have succumbed to twentieth-century redevelopment, just as the southern part of De Beauvoir Town did in the early 1960s.

Much of the northward expansion of Homerton from the mid-1830s was the work of William Bradshaw, who built a range of cramped terraces like Albert (later Wardle), Victoria and Brook (later Holmbrook) Streets, which had become slums by the 1860s, along with streets like College Street and Durham Place. South of the railway the sale of Sidney House led to its grounds being built over in the 1870s and Homerton linking up with South Hackney. Housing spread east of Brooksby's Walk in the 1880s. Glyn Road replaced Pratt's Lane and roads on the north side of the High Street at the junction with Marsh Hill in 1881, where Pincey Street had

Haywood's Buildings lay at the southern end of Fenn Street (Homerton High Street is on the other side of the arch). Probably named after John Haywood, a local baker, they were built in the 1820s and were cleared to build the western part of the Bannister House estate shortly after 1931.

been constructed on the west side of the site of Tower Place's moat by 1893. Some streets to the south of the High Street, like New Cut (today's Link Street and dating from the early nineteenth century), rapidly descended into poverty but social change was also affecting former residential houses on the main road itself. The former Sedgewick house by Ram's Episcopal church became a pawnbroker's in the late 1860s; Eagle House was taken by a dyer in about 1887. Rebuilding replaced older ranges, like the Plough and its adjoining properties, which had all gone by 1887. The former Upper Homerton, now Urswick Road, was affected by the opening of the truant school, which was enlarged by the demolition of the former Rivaz family home in 1905 and by industrialization, culminating in the building of Barlow's Metal Box factory north of Sutton Place in 1903.

But it was Hackney Wick that became the poorest area. In 1879 six thousand people were housed in very poorly constructed housing that had been built on rubbish where brick-earth had been excavated. It was said to house those who had sunk to the lowest depths. The area had attracted a number of noxious industries which felt themselves at a sufficient distance from prying local officials. Even though some back-to-back cottages were demolished in the 1890s, by the turn of the century infant mortality was the highest in Hackney.

Development in Lower Clapton included 'respectable' streets, like Laura Place, built by 1842, but the area was affected by the development of north Homerton and by the construction of the East London Union workhouse and the Eastern Fever hospital. The Hall and Priory House estate was sold in 1860 and bought by the London Suburban Land and Development Company. It also acquired the neighbouring Alderson estate and laid out Chatsworth Road, together with Glenarm, Clifden and the other streets of the Clapton Park estate from 1867 to

Powerscroft Road, with part of Clapton Park Congregational Church (on the right). Photograph, Alfred Braddock, 1905.

Cromwell Lodge (set back from the road) and Durham House, shortly before demolition. Photograph, Alfred Braddock, 1886.

1873. The Alderson house made way for Clapton Park chapel – the Round chapel – in 1869. Development saw the rebuilding of much of the High Road in the 1880s and the Powells sold off Durham House and Cromwell Lodge on the west side, together with Pond Lane nursery for building from 1882. Further south the last of the Five Houses on Lower Clapton Road went in 1884 for the construction of Lesbia Road (itself redeveloped in the 1970s). A symbol of further changes to come was the construction of two purpose-built blocks of flats in the north-eastern corner of Clapton Square in 1899 to 1901.

Upper Clapton and Stamford Hill were being deserted by the very wealthy middle classes from the 1840s but the process of social change was slower. While most of the land between Clapton Common and Hackney Downs had been built over by 1894, some by builders who had been active in the development of Stoke Newington, like William Osment, Clapton Common itself was still separated by private grounds from the summit of Stamford Hill. Craven Lodge had been left empty when philanthropist Samuel Morley, who had bought it from the Craven family, left in 1870. After his departure the estate was gradually developed by Reuben Button, although the lodge was not demolished until 1904. Redevelopment of the large houses on Stamford Hill was under way from the 1880s and new developments included a mixture of flats and cottages at Gibson Buildings (now Gibson Gardens) in Northwold Road in 1892.

By the end of the nineteenth century Hackney was perceived as having grown poorer over the last half-century. There were sections of poor housing in all areas of the parish, although the north remained more open and more prosperous, with London businessmen remaining in Upper Clapton and Stamford Hill. Many of the older houses on the main roads had been demolished for the construction of new streets, or had survived in institutional use. But although there were unhealthy riverside cottages and some very crowded courts and alleys, the patches of real poverty were comparatively small, concentrated round the factories near London Fields, Homerton and Hackney Wick. In 1901 23.1 per cent of the population was in total poverty – half the figure of Bethnal Green to the south – and the death rate was a little above the London average. But there was already the beginning of overcrowding in the southern area and this was to grow worse with a wave of new immigration in the first decade of the twentieth century.

As part of the process of development there were also changes in Hackney's transport system. In 1825 there were twelve short-stage coaches making forty-four return journeys between London and Clapton, Hackney, Homerton and Stamford Hill. Dickens recorded a slow journey to the Swan on Clapton Common in *Sketches by Boz*, originally published in 1833. By 1838 there

Kendall's coach waits outside the White Swan on Clapton Common while horse traffic bustles by. From a painting by Pollard, 1853.

London Fields station, *c.* 1900.

were fourteen buses running to Hackney and Clapton with a further one each to Dalston and Kingsland. In 1849, on the eve of the arrival of the railway, ten firms provided over seventy return journeys between Clapton and the City and another firm offered a quarter-hourly service from Church Street. There were buses between Homerton and Camberwell, Homerton and the West End and services from Stamford Hill via Islington to the Bank. Seven carriers offered collection from named shops, public houses and post offices. In 1856 some fifty-two vehicles were bought from local operators by a company that became the London General Omnibus Company in 1858, and which provided the majority of Hackney's bus services in 1901.

But it was the advent of the railway in 1850, followed by the establishment of tram services in the 1870s, which put Hackney in easy reach of the City for some of the army of clerks that had made a major contribution to the growth of the area. Hackney's first railway connection was established in 1850 when the East and West India Docks and Birmingham Junction Railway opened, with stations at Kingsland and Hackney. The company was renamed the North London Railway Company in 1853 and opened a station at Victoria Park in 1856. From 1854 the line was linked with the Eastern Counties Railway at Stratford. The course of the line south of Homerton was a further factor in the social decline of that area. The NLR was taken over by the London and North Western Railway in 1909. Later alterations included the opening of a new line to Broad Street in 1866, with a new station at Dalston Junction. The Victoria Park station was re-sited and a new station opened at Homerton in 1868. Hackney's station moved from the east to the west side of the road in 1870. The Great Eastern Railway built a new branch north from Bethnal Green through Hackney to the west of Mare Street. This opened in 1872, with stations at London Fields, Hackney Downs and on the Enfield branch at Rectory Road and Stamford Hill. Stoke Newington Common was cut in two by the Enfield branch but local pressure was able to ensure that the Chingford line tunnelled under Hackney Downs when it opened in 1873, providing a station at Clapton.

Horse tram at Upper Clapton ready to set off for Moorgate. Photograph, Alfred Braddock, 1879.

The short-lived North London Tramways Merryweather steam tram climbs towards Stamford Hill near the Ravensdale Road junction, *c.* 1885.

Electric tramcars at Mare Street. Photograph, Alfred Braddock, *c.* 1907.

The North Metropolitan Tramways Company established the first horse-drawn tram route in 1872, along Kingsland Road up to Stamford Hill. The following year a line from Bishopsgate ran via Haggerston to Mare Street and Lower Clapton and was extended in 1875 to Clapton Common. Two further lines, from Dalston to Mare Street, and from Bethnal Green through Victoria Park to Cassland Road, opened in 1875 and 1879 respectively. Depots were at the end of Bohemia Place and from 1873 at Portland Avenue. The Lea Bridge, Leyton and Walthamstow Tramway opened in stages from 1883, completing a section from Clapton to Lea Bridge in 1892. With the brief exception of a steam service on the Stamford Hill route run by the North London Tramways Company between 1884 and 1891, all services remained horse-drawn at the time the LCC took over the North Metropolitan's lease in 1906. Electrification was begun in 1907 and Hackney's last tram ran in March 1939.

Hackney's population was 31,047 in 1831 and grew to only 37,771 ten years later, but thereafter there were steep rises to 53,589 in 1851, 76,687 in 1861, 115,110 in 1871, and 163,681 in 1881. Growth rates then slowed with the population standing at 198,606 in 1891 and 219,272 in 1901.

Hackney's select and open vestries were merged into one in 1833. Anglican church and local government finance continued to be closely linked. Church rates were levied on all ratepayers, though protests against them increased in the 1830s. In April 1833 a dispute led to no rate being levied and when the congregation arrived at St John at Hackney they found that the churchwardens had suspended a number of parish officers, including the beadle and the organist. The service proceeded as normal 'except that when the clergyman . . . retired to prepare for the communion, instead of the usual singing of psalms, a perfect silence reigned, which threw great gloom over the congregation'. Church rates survived until 1866.

The women's ward in H Block of Hackney union workhouse, *c.* 1900.

Maintaining the poor was no longer in parochial hands. In 1824 the Poor Law Amendment Act vested responsibility in the Hackney Poor Law union, which combined Hackney and Stoke Newington. The old Hackney workhouse was demolished and replaced by a new building completed in 1842. This work was undertaken by Hackney's Trustees of the Poor, who continued to exist as a rating body, though they sold the new workhouse to the Union in 1845. By 1849 the Homerton site included a chapel, an infirmary, a stone yard, and schools, which came in for substantial criticism in 1854. The workhouse was expanded again, when it absorbed the southern part of Homerton Castle's grounds to the east in the 1860s and the house site itself in 1879 for a new infirmary. Both able-bodied and infirm paupers were housed there in 1885 when the workhouse held 1,090 inmates. By then workhouse children were sent out to Brentwood, where the Hackney union had taken sole control of a school built for Shoreditch in 1854. There was also a children's home at Ongar. The harshest conditions had been relaxed a little by the early 1890s, with old men allowed to smoke and some old couples allowed to live together, but substantial trouble was to come. The infirmary became overcrowded in 1893 and then in the following year cruelty to children was reported at Brentwood. The scandals led to the replacement of many of the board members and the election of the first woman members in 1895. The workhouse survived until 1930, when its buildings became part of Hackney Hospital. The LCC improved the old buildings and opened a nurses' home on the side of the site next to Sidney Road in 1937. In 1968 the hospital had 920 beds and was already outdated but the situation had worsened by 1976 when one ward block was described as 'arguably the worst general psychiatric facility in the country'. But cuts to the building programme at the new Homerton Hospital delayed closure and Hackney Hospital remained in use for geriatric and psychiatric patients until 1993.

Hackney's vestry had lost control of the poor law and some change followed with a highways board set up in 1836, though the lamp board created in 1763 and challenged in the 1830s continued to be responsible for street lighting until 1856. The first major watershed came in 1855, when the Metropolis Local Management Act established a new vestry with 119 members, one third of whom were elected annually. The new vestry had more limited functions than the old but superseded the three former Hackney vestries established in 1831 for all but strictly church functions. The vestrymen elected members to a district board of works and, combined with Stoke Newington, sent one member to London's local government created under the same act, the Metropolitan Board of Works. Initially the new bodies met in Hackney's town hall, a one-storey building put on the site of Urswick's house in 1802 and later given a top floor, but in 1866 the district board and the trustees of the poor combined to finance the construction of a new town hall. This building, in the middle of the open space on Hackney Grove, was completed in 1866 and later extended in 1899. The old town hall was leased to a number of bodies, including the poor law guardians and several provident societies. Part was occupied by the London City and Midland Bank from 1899. Stone clad in 1900 the building remains in bank use today.

Hackney's Board of Works met weekly from 1855 and took over the work of the former highway and lighting boards. Its officers included a clerk, a surveyor, an inspector of nuisances and a medical officer of health. The Board were lucky in their first medical officer, John William Tripe, but they were also enlightened enough to make a full-time appointment, rather than the part-timers employed by other London boards and vestries. Drainage was a major issue of the day. The rise in the number of buildings had turned Hackney Brook into an open sewer. Parts had already been culverted over but in 1859–60 the Metropolitan Board of Works completed a high-level sewer on the line of the brook as far as Church Street, and then south-east across Victoria Park down to Old Ford. The local Board was responsible for ensuring that drains from old and newly constructed houses were up to standard and for paving and clearing nuisances. The drainage records constitute Hackney's first record of building control. Before 1866 Hackney's staff was too small to carry out inspections

John William Tripe, Hackney's medical officer of health from 1855 to 1892. Tripe, who was active in public health matters that went far beyond Hackney and who attracted attention from Europe and America, died two weeks after leaving office.

unless there was a complaint, although in 1858 alone Tripe was able to report that 1,518 houses had been linked to the sewers and 1,839 nuisances abated. The 1866 Sanitary Act increased powers of inspection and Hackney was one of the first parishes to inspect all houses with a rental value of under £20 per annum.

But Tripe had to proceed with caution, since he was employed by the vestry, many of whose members owned rented-out property in Hackney. He also had to rely on his sanitary inspectors, who were largely unqualified. However the smallpox outbreak of 1883 gave Tripe the excuse to increase his rate of house inspection and his team checked up to 30,000 homes. By 1885 Tripe claimed he had inspected 20 per cent of Hackney's dwellings, including middle-class homes, where opposition is likely to have been fiercest. But this period of activity was short-lived as additional legislation imposed a greater workload by 1890 and the Public Health Act of 1891 added the inspection of over 2,000 factories to the work of the medical officer of health. In 1901 inspection of cow houses and slaughterhouses followed, though there was also an increase of staff to meet the new demands. The vestry was also reluctant to back up a rigorous inspection period after the small pox epidemic had subsided.

It was not just the growth of housing that posed problems for the Board of Works. In 1871 a *Hackney Gazette* reporter visited Daveys' Chemical Works on the Hackney Cut by Homerton Bridge. The works processed tar and had caused complaints for miles around. The reporter found

> piles of tarry casks and tubs and old boilers and a hundred other objects, black and stinking, lying about in all directions. Stills and furnaces send forth their fumes in far too great abundances and on the outer boundary is a 'tank' or reservoir of filthiness, open and exposed to atmospheric action that constitutes a host of dangers in itself. On the canal were lying sluggishly about a dozen barges embedded in murky slime . . . coloured with the rainbow-gorgeous tints, the emanations of exuded tar. . . . While the tall chimneys vomit forth their fumes, there is another evil constantly at work below. Streams of water with poisonous stuff dissolved within them are allowed to escape and passing underground for about a couple of hundred yards reappear in an open drain. . . . The drain in turn links to the sewer in Wick Lane, killing anything in the water. Residents complain of sickly children and adults with headaches, loss of appetite, with water in open cisterns frequently covered with slimy iridescent matters.

Several hundred people signed a petition to the Board to have the works removed. On a lighter note local people sometimes took direct action on local health problems. One Sunday afternoon in February 1878 'a large rat measuring twelve and a half inches was seen composedly crossing Well Street into Havelock Road [near Frampton Park Road] just as members of congregations were returning home from church and chapel. A chase was started by the men and boys and the rodent took refuge up the leg of the trousers of Mr Bright, a nearby resident, who immediately killed it.'

Stoke Newington had been dissatisfied with the merger with Hackney from the beginning and succeeded in having the district board abolished in 1894. For six years Hackney reverted to vestry government, with the trustees of the poor still raising money for the union, until both bodies were abolished by the Local Government Act of 1899 which created Hackney Metropolitan Borough Council for the new century. Probably the largest single project of the

Victoria Park's boating lake. Photograph, George James, *c.* 1870.

vestry years was the opening of Hackney's first publicly funded baths on Lower Clapton Road in 1897. The baths incorporated temporary flooring, which could turn one of the pools into a public hall, and in the 1990s the name 'King's Hall' has been revived for the refurbished baths, pool and leisure centre.

The creation of Victoria Park arose from two Acts of 1841 and 1842, which used money from the sale of York (later Lancaster) House to create a public park on the borders of South Hackney and Bethnal Green, and which came into use in 1846. It had been intended to allow up to a quarter of the land to be leased for building, though this was later reduced with a twenty-four-acre purchase by the MBW. In 1851 the park passed from the Commission of Woods and Forests to the Office of Works and Public Buildings and in 1887 to the MWB and its successors, the LCC and the GLC. A brief period of joint management by LB Hackney and Tower Hamlets ensued, after the abolition of the GLC in 1986, but when this broke up Tower Hamlets assumed the full management of the park. Boundary alterations in 1994 placed it wholly within Tower Hamlets.

Much of Hackney's commons and Lammas land had survived to the mid-nineteenth century as open land but it was still used for agricultural purposes. When the tenant of Hackney Downs failed to gather in his hay crop by Lammas in 1837, one parishioner exercised his right to let his cows loose on the land and another seized part of the crop. A case against both failed but led to false rumours that the Downs was public property and a crowd of over 3,000 despoiled it. But it was an attempt to build on London Fields in the early 1860s that raised the real spectre of the loss of the land. Hackney District Board used the Metropolitan Commons Act of 1866 to organize a petition to enclose just under 180 acres of common land, and this land was successfully transferred to the MBW in 1872. The transferred land included Clapton Common, Stoke Newington Common, Millfields, Hackney Downs, Well Street Common, London Fields and small roadside strips in Dalston Lane and Grove Street, South Hackney. But the enclosure did not extinguish all rights. While the lord of the manor did not uphold his agent's gravel-digging activities on Stoke Newington Common in 1875, he did insist on enclosing parts of Hackney Downs and Millfields; the Grocers' Company did the same on Hackney Downs in 1877 while their new school was under construction. The MWB lost a case against the lord of the manor and the matter was only resolved in successive purchases of rights by them in 1881 and the remaining freeholders in 1884. This left Hackney Marshes, which were in greater grazing use and did not pass to the LCC until 1893. Hackney's last park, Springfield, was the result of a public campaign, one of whose officers was resident in one of the three houses owning ground that went to make Springfield Park, bought from the Bros family in 1904.

Water supply remained a problem through the nineteenth century. New filter beds were built at Lea Bridge by the East London Waterworks Company in 1853, with further beds built on the Essex side in 1867. Hackney's vestry was in favour of a public body to improve water in 1850 and even thirty-eight years later the New River Company was unable to provide a constant supply to the parts of Hackney it served – the north-west corner of the parish, Shacklewell, Dalston and De Beauvoir Town – while there were failures in the East London Company's supply in 1894. But London had to wait until 1904 until the companies were abolished and the Metropolitan Water Board took over water supply.

The expanding population put pressure on the local Anglican churches. The local committee formed under the auspices of the rector J.J. Watson in 1839 found that in the part of Hackney that remained after the detachment of West and South Hackney, less than a fifth of the potential congregation could be accommodated. The committee was promised some funds from the church building commissioners and the Bishop of London. They also raised much more locally so that St James church, Clapton, and St Philip's, Dalston, were both consecrated in 1841, along with St Peter's, De Beauvoir Town, built on land donated by Richard Benyon de Beauvoir. St Barnabus, Homerton, was completed in 1847. Eight further churches followed between 1866 and 1872: St Michael and All Angels, London Fields (1865), St Augustine's, Victoria Park (1867), Christ Church, South Hackney (1871), St Matthew's, Mount Pleasant (1869), Christ Church, Rendlesham Road (1871), St Mark's Dalston (1860 iron church, 1870 present church) and St Luke's, Homerton (1872). A new parish church for South Hackney dedicated to St John of Jerusalem replaced the former chapel of ease in 1848. Hackney's seven other Anglican churches were completed in the next two decades, with the last new church, St Barnabas, Shacklewell, finished in 1910 but not consecrated until 1929. Some of these churches had developed out of mission activity in the poorer districts of Hackney, notably St Mary at Eton, which had its origins in a mission established over an undertaker's shop in Mallard Street in 1880. Until 1918 all the clergy were old Etonians. The church, on the site of a former ropeworks on the west side of Gainsborough Road, was completed in 1892, with the gate tower to the adjoining mission buildings being completed in 1912. Both were a visible sign of the triumph of the mission over considerable local hostility and indifference. The ties with Eton College were not severed until 1973.

Hackney's nonconformist churches also expanded in the nineteenth century. Some existing congregations split, resulting in new churches like Pembury Grove chapel in Lower Clapton of 1851, but there was substantial expansion by groups like the Baptists. They established eighteen congregations after 1830, including the Downs congregation, whose church was built in 1868–9. Hackney's first Methodists took over the meeting place in Shore Place, which the Baptists left empty when they moved to Mare Street in 1812; this congregation later built a church on Richmond Road in 1865. Between them the branches of Methodism established twenty-one places of worship, some short-lived. The last was Hackney Central Hall, completed in 1925 to replace the Richmond Road chapel. It became the headquarters of the Hackney mission and included halls, a gymnasium and ground-floor shops. In 1979 it was sold to LB Hackney, though with the shops retained for use by the mission, and went on to house Hackney's Museum and the music library. Both have vacated the building at the time of writing and it is in the course of being converted into a centre for the performing arts, funded in part by a lottery grant and incorporating the former Central Library next door.

General William Booth (founder of the Salvation Army) was a Hackney resident for many years, first at Cambridge Lodge Villas from 1865–7 (whose site is now part of St Joseph's Hospice); at no. 3 Gore Road from 1868–80 (after which it became the army's first training home); and then to Clapton Common. In 1882 he opened the converted former London Orphan Asylum as Congress Hall, including training barracks and Hackney's largest place of worship in 1903. Other premises used or owned by the Army included the former Glenarm Road theatre, mission halls in Hackney Wick, Well Street, Almack Road and a citadel at Cambridge Heath. The army also founded a maternity hospital, later known as the Mothers' Hospital. Originally intended for unmarried women, it opened at the Ivy House on the corner of Mare Street and Richmond Road in 1894, but moved to the former Maitland Place on Lower Clapton Road in 1912. It closed in 1986.

The local German community had their own Hamburg Lutheran church near the German Hospital, funded by compensation when the former church in Great Trinity Lane was demolished by the Metropolitan District Railway Company. It opened in 1876 in Ritson Road on a site next to the German Hospital. It closed before 1983 and the building is now used by a Pentecostal church. Hackney and adjoining parts of north-east London had acquired a substantial German community by the 1870s. But the German Hospital dated from 1845, when it took over the houses formerly used by the Dalston Orphan Asylum. The intention of the founders had been to create a hospital supported by subscription but free to Germans or German speakers; however, the majority of patients were poor English from the early days. A new building opened in 1864, with a new entrance from Ritson Road from 1877. German staff were returned after the First World War but internments from 1939 broke the German link. The hospital was dealing with psychiatric and psychogeriatric patients in 1974 and was closed in 1987.

Hackney's most unusual congregation was undoubtedly the Agapemonites. Followers of Henry James Prince built the Church of the Ark of the Covenant at the corner of Rookwood and Castlewood Roads in 1893–5. Large

The Hamburg Lutheran Church, Ritson Road, seen from the gates of the German Hospital, c. 1885.

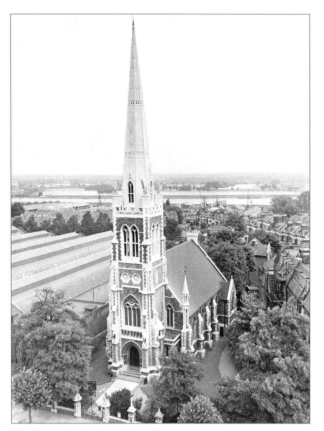

The former Agapemonite Church of the Good Shepherd, Rookwood Road, photographed from Tower Court, 1969.

beasts of the Evangelists adorn the corners at the base of the spire and within there are spectacular windows with artwork by Walter Crane. In 1902 Prince's successor, John Hugh Smyth-Pigott, was enthroned at the church, claiming to be the new Messiah, resulting in the attendance of a large and hostile crowd and a near riot. The church survived local hostility but had ceased to be used for worship in the 1920s. It was leased to the Ancient Catholic Church in 1956, whose rites include spiritual healing, and remains in use today.

Jewish immigration from what is now Tower Hamlets brought the local population up to perhaps five thousand Jews by 1880 and there were further arrivals from Poland and Russia in the next three decades. Three synagogues were established in Hackney before 1900 – the Dalston synagogue (in 1874 on Ridley Road, though moving to Mildmay Road two years later), Hackney Synagogue, begun in 1881 but established at Devonshire (now Brenthouse) Road in 1892, and the Stoke Newington Synagogue (begun as the New Dalston in 1887 and whose new building on the site of the Limes, Shacklewell Lane, opened in 1903). The Stoke Newington synagogue closed in 1976 and became one of Hackney's mosques in 1990.

Hackney had three hospitals other than those covered above. The Eastern Hospital was one of the first three 'isolation' foundations of the Metropolitan Asylum Board and opened in 1871 to cater for smallpox and fever cases. An ambulance station had been built on the site by 1889 and the site was enlarged by the purchase of the adjoining London institution (originally the East London workhouse) in 1921. The Eastern was enlarged in 1935 but a planned rebuilding in 1939 was halted by the war. The hospital closed before 1981 and the site was cleared for the new Homerton Hospital, which opened in 1986. The Metropolitan Free Hospital moved to a site on the west side of Kingsland Road, south of St Peter's Road, in 1886. It was intended for a poor area but only treated subscribers and was under-used in 1888, though fees on all beds had been abolished by 1935. It closed in 1977. It is now used as the Metropolitan Workshops, with the nurses' home at the rear converted into flats in the mid-1990s.

8. SOCIABLE & CHARITABLE

Confiding in his diary in 1716, the young Dudley Ryder felt that there was little to do in the Hackney of his day and 'no sociableness or familiarity kept up between families'. Outside the family houses the oldest places of entertainment were the inns. Hackney had seven in 1552 and in 1636 a poet named three, the King's or Prince's Arms at Kingsland and the Mermaid and the Rose in Hackney village. Premises could lose their licences: one victualler lost his in 1639 because of his wife's bad character and the landlord at Temple Mills quarrelled with Henry Rowe in 1686. Some seventeenth-century taverns issued tokens and these record a Chequers at Kingsland in 1663, the Flower de Luce at Clapton and six others in Hackney village besides the Mermaid, including the Cock in 1651, the Magpie in 1656 and the Green Man in 1667. Parochial business was conducted at the Flying Horse in 1708 and the Mermaid in 1710, which was probably where Pepys had eaten cherries and played shuffleboard in 1664, but the vestrymen also met in coffee houses. There were two in Church Street in 1719, one of which may have become the Hackney coffee house owned by Sir John Silvester, which survived, along with a coffee house at Shacklewell present in 1785, to about 1800.

There were just under 60 licences granted in eighteenth-century Hackney, increasing to 85 in 1849 and over 250 by 1872. Most were on the main roads, though there were two near the marsh gate at Homerton, one at Shacklewell, one by one of the ferries (probably that

The Horse and Groom, Lea Bridge. Watercolour by C.Bigot, *c.* 1830.

replaced by Lea Bridge) and one at Temple Mills. Some of the older establishments had their own pleasure grounds. The Sun on the west side of Church Street had its own bowling green in 1698 and skittles were played at the Plough in Homerton in 1785. There was also a bowling green on a site south-west of Meeting Field Path, which Dudley Ryder patronized in 1716. The tea gardens at the Red Cow in Dalston Lane were later built over but some pubs kept their grounds until the 1860s, like the Three Compasses in Dalston Lane, while the riverside gardens of the Horse and Groom at Lea Bridge in 1821 and the Mount Pleasant at High Hill ferry in 1838 were popular with fishermen and boating parties.

Hackney's best known gardens were those of the new Mermaid on the west side of Church Street, using the grounds of the former rectory house and part of the glebe field. In 1810 there was a trap-ball ground and in 1842 space for archery. The grounds were available for larger gatherings, like the outdoor benefit feast held by the Licensed Victuallers Association in 1832 to fund their school. Balloon ascents were popular in the early nineteenth century and included trips by James Sadler in 1811 and by Mrs Graham and two other women in 1836. An ascent in 1822 was accompanied by fireworks, among which was 'a boa constrictor in pursuit of a butterfly and the grand illuminated temple'. There was an assembly room at the rear of the new Mermaid, probably opened after 1716 and kept by a Mr Holmes before 1744. One of Holmes's successors, Antony Brunn, who took on the lease in 1766, rebuilt the assembly rooms and advertised seasonal Wednesday balls there in 1778 and 1780. The new Mermaid was demolished before 1845 to make way for J.R.D. Tyssen's Manor House but the assembly rooms survived. Approached by a narrow passage to the north of the Manor House, they acquired the former new Mermaid's singing and dancing licences and were used by the Hackney Literary and Scientific Society in 1870. The rooms were sold in 1877 and rebuilt to include a large concert hall and a skating rink on what remained of the gardens to the south. This in turn had gone by 1894, replaced by Kenmure Avenue and the Manor cinema. There was another assembly room at the rear of the former Templars' House, known as the Blue Posts inn and run by Thomas Wright from 1760–85. The artist John Varley was said to have been born there in 1778 at a time when his father had converted it back to a private house.

Francis Tyssen licensed three waits in his manorial capacity in 1704, as an attempt to control revelry that had got out of hand. It had been the nonconformists that had banned the strolling players at the Old Mermaid in 1768 and opposed puppet showmen. In 1778 a request for actors to put on a performance for two nights at the Blue Posts was refused and in 1824 the vestry asked the magistrates not to license any theatres in the parish. But there were musical performances at inns and the Luxembourg Hall (facing down Ashwin Street) and the Albion Hall on Albion Square were used for amateur dramatic performances. The second Three Colts in Grove Street was licensed in 1863 and was known as Scott's Music Hall before it was closed for failing to keep legal hours in 1875.

Hackney's first theatre was built for Thomas Turner and designed by J.T. Robinson behind nos 79–81 Glenarm Road. It opened before 1875 and was known successively as the Hackney theatre, the Theatre Royal, the Clapton Park theatre and latterly as 'the old dust hole', but it lasted only until 1884 when the building was taken as the first Clapton Park tabernacle. Rather more successful was the Hackney Empire, designed by Frank Matcham for Oswald Stoll at nos 381–91 Mare Street and opened in 1901. It held over three thousand people and was home to many famous acts before its closure in 1956. It was used as a television studio before being bought by Mecca Ltd to serve as a bingo hall. The statue of Euterpe that topped the central pediment had already gone in 1979 when Mecca removed the pediment and the flanking terracotta domes. The resulting enquiry and public pressure secured the restoration of the domes and while work was in progress Mecca conveyed the Hackney Empire to a preservation trust, whose leading light was Roland Muldoon. The theatre re-opened in 1986; the domes, pediment and Euterpe were restored in 1988 and the Empire is now one of the most successful local theatres in London, hosting many of the alternative comedy stars in the 1980s and 1990s.

Impressions of the proposed Hackney Empire by its architect Frank Matcham, 1900.

Feathers galore at the Hackney Empire, February 1934.

The Hackney Empire had also been used as a cinema from 1910. One of Hackney's earliest cinemas had been opened in the previous year by Edward Mason who ran a cinematograph exhibition at no. 329 Mare Street. The Clapton Premier skating rink opened in December 1909 but had been converted to a cinema in 1910. Other conversions were more curious. In 1912 the former St Thomas Square chapel opened as the Empress cinema, which was rebuilt as the Essoldo in 1937. It became a bingo hall in the 1960s and was demolished in 1996 for the construction of a new residential block for Cordwainer's College. Another early theatre was the Kingsland Palace on no. 105 Kingsland High Street. Opened in 1909, it was replaced by the Kingsland Empire occupying nos 103–5 in 1915. This in turn was rebuilt as the smaller Classic in 1937 and was one of Hackney's last commercial cinemas when it closed in 1975. It became a residents' centre and then, in 1982, the Rio, a community cinema. The Dalston Palace of Varieties on the south side of Dalston Lane opened in 1898 but became the Dalston Picture Theatre by 1912 and the Dalston Picture House from 1920. It was the Dalston Gaumont by 1958 and closed as a cinema before 1964. Latterly it was an Afro-Caribbean club, the Four Aces, but

The Premier skating rink, Lower Clapton Road, probably taken before the opening in December 1909.

The Hackney Pavilion, Mare Street, 1955.

at the time of writing is closed, awaiting demolition, as part of the redevelopment of much of the south-west end of Dalston Lane. The splendid Hackney Pavilion, designed by George Billings and seating 1,162, opened at no. 290 Mare Street in 1914. In the 1950s it had a very active children's club but it became a victim of declining local cinema audiences and after showing *Carry On At Your Convenience*, perhaps an appropriate injunction, it closed in 1973. The site is now a bank and council offices.

A range of grander cinemas opened from the mid-1920s, including the Regent on the corner of Stamford Hill and Amhurst Park seating 2,182 in 1925; the Regal, on the corner of Well Street and Mare Street on the former Polikoff factory site in 1936; the Odeon at no. 505a Kingsland Road and the Ritz next to the Kenning Hall on Lower Clapton Road, both in 1939. But all cinemas were in decline from the mid-1950s. The twelve survivors of 1958 were down to seven in 1964. The Regal and the Odeon closed before 1975; the latter had a brief revival but closed again and the building was demolished in the mid-1980s to make way for sheltered accommodation. The Ritz closed before 1975 and its neighbour the Kenning Hall in 1979, though the building survives as a nightclub. The Regal, renamed the Mare Street ABC and then the Mayfair, closed in 1981. After a period as a bingo hall, it was briefly revived as a cinema but when business did not meet costs, it was converted to club use.

The River Lea and Hackney Marshes offered a range of sporting opportunities. There was horse racing on both the Hackney Downs and the marshes in 1733, with customers to the latter getting free shares in an ox roast provided by Thomas Rudge, a brewer. In 1737 two horses swam from Tylers ferry to Lea Bridge. There were also crueller sports. In 1788 a pig was shaved, had its tail greased and 'was turned out to be caught by any person, who holding it by the tail and throwing it over his head, was entitled to a gold laced hat'. In 1791 bull baiting was mixed with prize fighting on the marshes before a crowd of 3,000 people. John Baum, the landlord of the White Lion at Hackney Wick from about 1825, made use of adjoining land to provide a boxing ring and used land to the north of the pub to set up a running track. One race was run between a series of English champions and Deerfoot, an American Indian in 1863. Deerfoot lost the contest but Baum named a row of cottages he was building in Hackney Wick in his honour. The running track was sold off after 1871 and Bartripp Street built on the site. As late as 1875 a man was killed in an informal boxing match on the marshes.

John Baum's promotion of the Deerfoot contest, 1863.

Refreshments on a boat racing day near the Robin Hood, River Lea, *c.* 1890. Photograph, Alfred Braddock.

George Grocott, Hackney's first town clerk, remembered mid-Victorian winters when the marshes flooded and then froze. Skaters holding lanterns and torches could enjoy miles of open, free skating. 'Tents and fires were to be observed here and there, while perhaps a party would find a nice clear piece of ice . . . for fancy skating and a waltz to the music of some itinerant musicians.' But they would also have to watch for muggers on skates, robbing the unwary who strayed away from company into the darkness. Part of the marsh was used by the Eton Mission for recreation; this land later became the Eton Manor boys' club sports ground. There had been problems with disputes between manorial drovers and boys from the Mission playing football in 1889, and the further possibility that the owners might sell the marshes for building led Hackney's district board to appeal to the LCC, which went on to acquire the marshes for use as football pitches in 1893.

The River Lea was famous for its fishing and boating. The White House at Tylers Ferry had a subscription fishery in 1810 and the Beresford family also ran fisheries from the Horse and Groom public house by Lea Bridge. There was angling at Mount Pleasant in 1838 but the increase of pollution from sewage gradually killed off the fish and was only partially remedied by the Lea Purification Act of 1886. There were local rowing clubs from the 1860s, with boatyards at the bottom of Spring Hill. There were many clubs, some amateur, some linked to businesses, like the Post Office. In 1921 the River Lea branch of the National Rowing Association, which included Hackney club members, travelled to Calais to take on and beat the French. Radleys had a boatyard on Waterworks Road at Lea Bridge; other yards included Megg's at Middlesex Wharf, Verdons and Tyrell's at Spring Hill. After the formation of the Lea Valley regional park in 1967, Radley's yard was taken over and converted to Springfield marina, which opened in 1969.

Local cricket, football and rugby clubs used Hackney Downs, Victoria Park and other open spaces. Some clubs were multi-purpose, for example, the Dalston Alberts were cricketers and rowers. Glyn Cricket Club spawned a football branch, which started in 1881 at Homerton College and played on open ground at Glyn Road in 1884. It became Orient in 1889 and Clapton Orient in 1903. The club turned professional in 1903 but after its ground was taken for dog-racing at the Clapton stadium in 1928, it moved to Lea Bridge and ultimately to Leyton in 1937, where it changed its name to Leyton Orient. Dog-racing at the stadium lasted until 1969, when the stadium was closed to make way for the Millfields estate. Hackney Wick stadium opened in 1932 and hosted both dog and motor cycle racing. Speedway was reintroduced in 1963. After a turbulent period in the 1990s the stadium also closed. Local gymnastic clubs included the

Hackney's Mayor, Cllr Saleem Siddiqui and officers of the Pickwick Bicycle Club at the unveiling of a plaque in 1995 to celebrate the 125th anniversary of the foundation of the club.

Orion, founded in Mile End in 1868 and which moved to a new hall in Casterton Street in 1883. This was acquired as a drill hall in 1912 and the club moved again, opening Orion Hall in 1914 in East Bank, which was still there in 1992. The Casterton Street hall was refurbished as the George Sylvester sports centre by the London Borough of Hackney and included courts for ball games and a rifle range. This centre closed in turn in 1991 and the activities moved to one of the disused pools in the Lower Clapton Road baths.

Hackney also had a range of cycling clubs, founded in the 1870s. One of the more unusual was the Pickwick Bicycling Club, founded in 1870 at the Downs Park Hotel. Membership was limited to numbers corresponding to the characters in *Pickwick Papers* and members collected period bicycles. The club, which claims to be the oldest bicycle club in Britain, celebrated the 125th anniversary of its foundation at the Downs in 1995.

Sporting activities were also linked to churches or religious instruction, like the Grove Young Men's Institute, founded in 1876 in a schoolroom of the Old Gravel Pit chapel before moving to Brooksby's Walk, where members could also use the library or engage in debates. In Hackney Wick the Eton Mission ran a boys' club in 1907 when an old Etonian working with the mission, Gerard Wellesley, decided to form a club for those over eighteen not catered for in the boys' club. The new club provided boxing and other sporting activities and a summer camp for Wick children at Eton College. The original club premises, the coal shop on Daintry Street and a successor on the corner of Gainsborough Road and Daintry Street, were soon outgrown and Wellesley helped acquire land next to Victoria Park station on a site bounded by Riseholme Street, the railway and the backs of houses in Cadogan Terrace in 1913. On this site, which had been part of the former Wick Hall dairy farm, a new club house and the 'Manor House' were built, the latter intended for visiting helpers and Wellesley himself. New facilities included a library, space for cricket and football, and an 'Urchins Club' for the under-fourteens. Wellesley needed to earn a living and left in 1922, replaced by Barings banker Arthur Villiers, who moved into the Manor House and ran the club until his death in 1969. Villiers acquired land in Leyton in 1923 and on 'The Wilderness' added football pitches, rugby and cricket grounds, tennis courts and a running track. Supporters of the club included his nephew Frank Pakenham, later Lord Longford. Villiers fought a proposal by Herbert Morrison for the LCC to acquire a large area of the Hackney Marshes for housing and although the club closed for the duration of the Second World War, it reopened in 1945. Final closure of the Hackney site came in 1967 in advance of its compulsory purchase for motorway construction and the trust established by Villiers continued educational work at Villiers Park, Middleton Stoney.

Other local societies included the Hackney Literary and Philosophical Society, founded in 1811 and probably short-lived, and the Hackney Reading Society, founded in 1815, which lasted until 1911. The Hackney Literary and Scientific Institution, founded in 1848, met in the Manor rooms from 1848 to 1894 and offered lectures, a library, entertainments and a range of

The anti-pacifist riot at the Brotherhood Church, Southgate Road, July 1917.

classes. The Hackney Choral Society of 1837 lasted only five years but was the forerunner of a number of local choral groups in being in the 1860s. Public halls were also available for recreation, including the largest, Morley Hall, at the Triangle, founded from Cambridge Heath Congregational Church in 1885 but in industrial use from 1924. Gardening societies included the exclusive horticultural society for the Stamford Hill area, founded in 1833, who often met at the house of its president, Arthur Craven, of Craven Lodge. Clapton Naturalists' Club, formed in 1886 with involvement from boys from Hackney Downs School, was the forerunner of the present London Natural History Society. Other long-lived clubs included the Hackney Photographic Society formed in 1889 which was still active in the early 1990s.

Political clubs included a Social Democratic Club, which met at the Lamb and Flag from 1881–2. The most active local branch was the Kingsland one whose activities in 1896 included a lecture programme, a Sunday school and summer outings for children to Rigg's Retreat at Chingford. The Hackney Radical Club existed in 1887 and its premises in Kenmure Road provided a headquarters for the Hackney Trades Council during the General Strike of 1926. The Revd Bruce Wallace established the Brotherhood church in Southgate Road in 1891. Wallace was a member of the Kingsland SDF branch from a Congregational background and advocated a mixture of Christianity and Marxism. The church ran a grocery and vegetable co-operative from nos 1 and 5 Downham Road from 1894, with members' dividends intended to purchase land for new communities. A conference of the Russian Social Democrats met at the church in May 1907: delegates included Lenin, Stalin, Gorky and Zinoviev. The church was also the scene of an anti-pacifist riot in July 1917 but survived into the mid-1930s. Hackney's Conservative Association existed in 1872 and a Liberal Association formed two years later, while ratepayers groups were active in De Beauvoir Town and Dalston in the 1880s.

Hackney became a multi-racial community from the 1950s and by the mid-1980s there existed a wide range of community associations. Hackney Community Action and the Hackney Ethnic Minorities Alliance represented a wide range of interests and there were separate associations for Cypriots, Turks, Muslims, African women, Hindus and Chinese. There have been many residents' groups and tenants associations, some, like the De Beauvoir Association, publishing local news-sheets. The Hackney Society was formed in 1969 as an amenity society with historical interests and the Friends of Hackney Archives were formed under Hackney Society auspices by Hackney Council's Archives Department in 1985, to serve as a history society for Hackney and a user group for the Archives Department.

Besides its parochial charities, Hackney has been home to a wide range of charitable bodies, some occupying old houses, others building their own premises. One such was Robinson's Retreat, founded by architect Samuel Robinson in 1812. Robinson had built a range of almshouses to his own design on the south side of Retreat Place, with a small garden opposite to house eight widows of Independent ministers and four widows of Baptists. The almshouses were let as flats in 1901 when the garden was built over and demolished after the Second World War. The Bakers' Company built almshouses in St Thomas Passage (now Lyme Grove) in about 1828, which closed in 1973. A benevolent society, the Goldsmiths' and Jewellers', built almshouses in Manor (later Holcroft) Road in 1853, which were demolished for the present Orchard Street school. Emanuel Pacifico left money that was used to establish Pacifico's almshouses for Sephardic Jews, housing about seven inmates on the south-east corner of London Fields and which opened in 1851. They were sold in 1897 and had been demolished by

Goldsmiths' and Jewellers' Asylum, Manor Road, *c.* 1853.

The French Hospital at Victoria Park Road, as drawn by D. Nanny and published in about 1850.

The London Orphan Asylum, with boys to the left and girls to the right of the central portico, 1860s.

1900. The Hand in Hand Asylum for Aged Jews occupied no. 23 Well Street in 1880 and lasted there until about 1907. Nos 23–5 later became Shuttleworth's Hotel.

Two other almshouses had religious associations. The hospital for French Protestants, founded in 1708, moved from its overcrowded and ancient buildings on Bath Street to a new building on the north side of Victoria Park, which opened in 1866. Housing sixty inmates, these buildings, designed by R.L. Roymieu, were Hackney's largest almshouse. After the hospital moved out in 1949 (it is now in Rochester), the premises became a convent school and are now part of Cardinal Pole school. There were Catholic almshouses built for forty poor Catholics, aged sixty or over from the gentry, professions or business. St Scholastica's Retreat – funded from the estate of Robert Harrison, who died in 1852, and his wife, Charlotte Scholastica – was built on the north side of the present Kenninghall Road in 1861–3. Designed by E.W. Pugin, the buildings existed until 1972.

There were a number of orphan asylums in Hackney. The grandest was the London Orphan Asylum, founded by Andrew Reed in 1813. The asylum was built on the former site of Hackney School on the east side of Lower Clapton Road in eight acres of ground and was completed in 1825. The asylum included a school for boys and girls and numbers rose from 206 in 1826 to about 440 in 1858. Both sexes had domestic duties, though the girls were expected to mend the boys' clothes. Housework by the children was paid for. The asylum appointed medical consultants and escaped the cholera outbreaks in 1849 and 1854 but there was a bad outbreak of typhoid in 1866, with 200 children affected and 15 deaths. The rural surroundings of the early days of the foundation had gone and in 1871 the children were moved to a new building on the edge of Watford. Briefly occupied by the Metropolitan Asylums Board

The sitting room of the Ayahs' Home, King Edward's Road, *c.* 1906.

from 1873–6, the former asylum was taken over by the Salvation Army from 1882 to 1970, when all but the central portico was demolished.

Other asylums included another Reed foundation, the Dalston Orphan Asylum, which moved to a house on Dalston Lane in 1832, and moved out to Essex in 1843, becoming the Royal Wanstead School. The three houses it occupied on closure were taken for the German Hospital. Women from the Refuge for the Destitute in Hoxton moved to the Manor House, Dalston Lane, in 1849; in 1924 the institution merged with the Elizabeth Fry Refuge for women prisoners, also founded in 1849. The Elizabeth Fry Refuge occupied the early eighteenth-century no. 195 Mare Street for over sixty years to 1913, when it moved to Highbury. Their Hackney base survives today as the last of the gentlemen's residences on Mare Street and is now home to the New Lansdowne Club. There were other orphanages run in association with the German Hospital (at no. 214 Dalston Lane from 1884 and later no. 106 Norfolk Road until 1939), the Anglican community of the Holy Childhood at no. 19 Clapton Common from 1897 to the Second World War, and by the Salvation Army at The Nest at no. 10 Springfield from 1902 into the 1930s.

Braidwood's school for the deaf was not the only institute for people with disabilities in the area. The British Asylum for Deaf and Dumb Females, founded by two ladies at Stamford Hill in 1851, had a brief sojourn in Eagle House, Homerton High Street, from 1857 to 1864, when it moved to the former Piss Pot Hall, no. 179 Lower Clapton Road. When that house was demolished for the Powell House estate in 1933, it moved again to no. 26 Clapton Common, until about 1986. The East London Home and School for Blind Children founded at no. 120 Lower Clapton Road in 1893 moved to nos 2–4 Warwick Road in 1902 and remained there until the building became a municipal welfare centre in about 1948.

Possibly Hackney's most extraordinary home was originally created by the London City Mission to provide a home for Indian servants brought over to England with their English employers. The Ayahs' Home started in Jewry Street in 1900; it moved to no. 26 King Edward's Road in 1900 where it lasted until wartime conditions brought about its closure in 1941.

9. FROM 1900

The population numbers peaked at 222,533 in 1911. Despite First World War casualties and the 1918 influenza epidemic, the population was 222,412 in 1921 but it fell to 215,333 in 1931 due to wartime disruption. Loss of housing and re-housing outside Hackney reduced the total to 171,342 in 1951. This decline continued with 164,766 people in 1961 and density down from 68 to 50 people per acre. Changes to ward boundaries under the London Borough of Hackney make comparisons with the pre-1965 figures impossible but LB Hackney's total population of 220,279 in 1971 fell to 180,434 in 1981. It is likely that the 1991 figure of 181,248 was artificially reduced by people seeking to evade poll tax registration.

Hackney began the new century as one of the metropolitan boroughs, consisting of a mayor, ten aldermen and sixty councillors for eight wards, altered in 1936 to eight aldermen and forty-eight councillors for sixteen wards. The council met in the town hall built by the vestry until 1937, though the gradual expansion in the council workforce necessitated its replacement in 1937 by the present town hall, behind the old one on the sites of houses in the former Hackney Grove. The council was initially controlled by the Conservatives, who as Municipal Reformers prevented Progressive control in 1906 by an alliance with members from the ratepayers' association. The local Labour Party, which grew out of the activities of the Hackney Trades Council formed in 1900, took control in 1919 but lost to a combination of Progressives and Reformers in 1922 and did not regain power until 1934. Thereafter the Labour group held the council and its successor from 1965, LB Hackney, until 1968, when a Conservative administration held power until 1972. Labour ran Hackney until after the 1994 election when disagreements in the Labour group culminated in a split in the party over investigations into the employment of a former social worker. Many councillors left the Labour Party and formed New Labour, which broke up as the 1998 elections approached, with members joining the Conservative and Liberal Democrat groups. The 1998 election saw Labour gaining twenty-nine seats, the Liberal Democrats seventeen, the Conservatives twelve and Hackney gaining its first two Green councillors in a ward contest that saw a former Labour leader of the council lose his seat.

Hackney gained its first two parliamentary seats in 1867. Liberals held both seats until the three constituencies of North, Central and South Hackney were formed in 1885, after which the North was Conservative until 1945, Central was Conservative until 1900, Liberal until 1923 and alternated between Conservative (1924, 1931) and Labour (1929) until Labour took it again in 1935. Hackney South was generally Liberal (though the Conservatives held the seat in 1895, 1900, 1922 and 1931). Labour took it in 1923 and in 1929, retaining it from 1935. The boundaries were changed in 1955, with the creation of the two seats of Hackney North and Stoke Newington and Hackney Central. Hackney South was merged with Shoreditch in the 1970s and LB Hackney had two seats for the 1982 election. Notable local MPs have included Sir Charles Reed (d. 1881), Chairman of the London School Board, his successor Henry

Fawcett (d. 1884), whose blindness did not interfere with a career that included the position of Postmaster General, and Herbert Morrison (d. 1965), who was co-opted as the second Labour Mayor of Hackney in 1920 and began his distinguished parliamentary career as MP for Hackney South in 1923. Much less reputable was the financier and jingoist Horatio Bottomley, who represented South Hackney from 1906, despite increasing local opposition, and stood as an independent in 1918 until his imprisonment in 1922. In 1889 another rogue, the journalist Frank Harris, author of the salacious *My Secret Life*, was adopted as South Hackney's conservative candidate, but fearing his adulterous affair would be discovered, and unwilling to visit his prospective constitu-ency, he resigned.

Hackney was joined with Shoreditch and Stoke Newington under the London Government Act of 1963 to form the London Borough of Hackney. A change in the composition of the local Labour Party in 1982 led to a range of organizational changes which introduced a directorate structure; this in turn was radically overhauled between 1997–8 under the Transforming Hackney initiative, which was a response to the long-perceived poor quality of many of Hackney Council's services.

Housing has proved to be one of the most significant areas of council activity in the century. Hackney Trades Council's attempts to get Hackney to adopt a municipal housing policy before the First World War were defeated by the successive Conservative and Progressive councils and their first municipal scheme of forty-eight maisonettes at Fletching Road, Millfields, was only completed in 1925. Further houses and maisonettes had been completed on Casimir Road and on the borders of Clapton Park by 1928. Major schemes followed round Southwold Road in 1930–2, on Lower Clapton Road when the Powell House estate was built in 1934 and at Homerton where the Bannister House estate of 1935 was further extended in 1960. The LCC also resumed its local building programme with the Shore estate of 1928–31, construction at Stamford Hill and five other estates under way by 1938. By 1939 Hackney Council was running thirteen estates. There were other pre-war providers, including the Samuel Lewis Trust and the Four Per Cent Industrial Dwellings Company, while the first housing association flats were built by the Bethnal Green and East London Association in Devonshire Road in 1931 and the Shoreditch Association in Loddiges Road in 1937.

Hackney between the wars remained principally residential, with 53 per cent of the working population being employed in London in 1921. But there were changes to privately owned housing, with the Cass trustees seeking to build flats to replace older housing and the Tyssen trustees letting property for trade purposes, notably dressmaking. Property damage during the Second World War provided the incentive for new council housing and of the 4,891 houses built by 1957, 2,816 were constructed by Hackney Council, 1,772 by the LCC and the remainder by private builders and housing associations. Hackney and the LCC had agreed a rough division of the borough, with the area south of the North London Railway seeing a concentration of LCC activity. In 1948 Hackney had said it would never build property above three storeys again but lack of space and changing fashions prompted the move to high-rise construction with eleven and fifteen storey blocks planned in 1960 and just under half of the twenty-two blocks of over sixteen storeys planned for LB Hackney as a whole between 1965 and 1967. But successful resistance by the Hackney Society in 1968 to a compulsory purchase order gradually began a change in housing policy, while changes in mortgage policy enabled owner occupiers to buy and then renovate older property. Conservative government constraints on local authority house construction saw the bulk of new construction in the 1980s being undertaken by housing associations, funded with government help through the Housing Corporation. Two of the most active of the local trusts were Circle Thirty Three and Newlon, both founded in 1968. Newlon was responsible for the redevelopment of the Mothers' Hospital site in the mid-1980s. By 1981 in the King's Park ward in Homerton nearly 95 per cent of the housing was council owned, though in seven wards the proportions were all under 50 per cent. Problems with poor maintenance led Hackney to demolish some of its older estates, like Powell House, replaced by a new estate in the early 1980s, and start demolishing some of the 1960s tower blocks, beginning with Northaid Point on the Trowbridge estate in 1985, which famously survived the first set of explosives. The largest redevelopment scheme to date, of the former Holly Street estate, is approaching completion in 1998.

An attempt to introduce a free public library in 1878 was defeated and it was left to the new metropolitan council to adopt the Public Libraries Act in 1903. The Mare Street library opened in 1908, with branches following at Dalston in 1912, Homerton and Clapton in 1914 and Stamford Hill in 1936. Dalston library was bombed in 1944 and replaced by the present building on Dalston Lane in 1959. Five other branches had been opened by 1951 and new libraries were built at Stamford Hill in 1968, Homerton in 1974, De Beauvoir Town (the Rose Lipman library) in 1975 and at Eastway in 1979. Successive closures reduced libraries in Hackney to five sites in 1998, with the lending library operating from a temporary site and the reference library in the former Rose Lipman library. Both services will go into a new library forming part of the Technology and Learning Centre, scheduled to be completed on a site south of the Reading Lane junction with Mare Street in the year 2000.

The new TLC will also house Hackney Museum, which opened in the former central hall in 1987. Hackney's archive and local history collections owe their origin to the collecting activities of the Tyssen family, whose archive was given to the vestry in 1885 and housed in the town hall. It passed to the new library in 1908 and was one of the first collections to come to Hackney Archives Department, formed in 1965 and housed from 1976 in the basement of the former Rose Lipman library. Despite its small size, Hackney Archives Department has developed a national reputation for quality of service, delivery and innovation in new technology. In 1998 its mapping, image and educational software, developed jointly between Information Sciences and the National Trust's Sutton House, was in the course of adoption by a number of other London local authorities and other authorities including the city of Birmingham.

Hackney opened five slipper baths between 1922 and 1935 and its first municipal laundry at Oldhill Street in 1958. All the former slipper baths and the majority of the laundries had closed by the end of the 1980s. Electric street lighting was first introduced in 1901, powered by a generating station at Millfields, with an adjacent refuse destructor to supply heat. Hackney was able to sell appliances and carry out domestic wiring from 1906. The plant passed to the London Electricity Board in 1947 and the bulk was demolished in the early 1980s. Millfields Road also housed a disinfecting station, dating from 1900, which saw heavy use in the 1930s as people's possessions were fumigated prior to being moved into new council housing. Public health functions were divided in 1974, with medical services passing to the National Health Service, who in 1985 ran seven health centres in Hackney. From 1965 social services became an increasingly important part of council expenditure, taking on residential, day care and a host of other functions. Hackney became an education authority in 1990.

The composition of Hackney's population changed substantially in the postwar period. Immigration in the 1930s laid the foundations of a strong Hassidic Jewish community in

Youth theatre and period costumes
in the panelled room of Sutton
House in 1994.

Stamford Hill and the creation of a number of religious organizations including the Lubavitch
Foundation, established in 1959. However the Jewish community in South Hackney diminished
from the 1970s with movement to other areas of North London. Immigration from the Indian
sub-continent and Turkey led to the establishment of mosques at no. 70 Cazenove Road in
1978, using the former Stoke Newington synagogue in 1981, at no. 2a Lea Bridge Road in 1984
(with a new building completed in 1991) and in the former Apollo cinema on Stoke Newington
Road in 1986. The 1950s saw the beginning of substantial immigration from the Caribbean and
in the 1970s of West Africans. By the early 1970s the intake of Jewish pupils at Hackney Downs
School was being outstripped by Afro-Caribbean boys. The largest concentration of Afro-
Caribbeans was in Hackney's central wards, including Dalston by the 1980s.

The 1980s saw important new environmental initiatives in Hackney. The creation of the
Dalston City Challenge task force in 1992, funded by the Department of the Environment, was
intended to regenerate the 'Dalston City Corridor' stretching along the Kingsland Road.
Planning for the centre of Hackney will create a new place for the performing arts and
a technology and learning centre, to add to the theatre programme of the Hackney Empire. To
the north the former Round chapel has also seen new life as performance and rehearsal space.
The renewal of Sutton House has brought in many visitors who would not otherwise have come
to Hackney. Elsewhere sales of council property and housing association schemes have removed
many of the derelict sites of the 1970s and 1980s. Despite campaigning that has gone on since the
1970s, Hackney still lacks its own tube line, though there is still the possibility of the conversion
of part of the former Broad Street railway line, closed in 1986 to form a tube link to Dalston.
Hackney has long been a place of incomers and has drawn on the energy and innovatory skills of
its peoples. In the coming century renewed links with the City of London and regeneration
initiatives should retain Hackney's reputation as a vibrant and surprising place in which to live.

INDEX

Illustrations indicated by bold type.